Praise for A BROAD ABR

"When this book was originally written, the word *expatriate* was not even in my vocabulary. After having spent nearly half of my life outside my native country, I'm so thankful to Robin Pascoe for putting this book back in print. It's full of timeless advice that trailing wives, expat mothers, and global broads everywhere will take to heart for years to come."
—*Danielle Barkhouse, author of The Expat Arc*

"This book changed my life. Reading it first after living abroad for ten years, I realized I wasn't mad to have been unhappy in paradise or wrong to be angry that I had sacrificed my professional identity and support network for my husband's job. Anyone reading this book for the first time will feel less alone and perfectly normal, and also learn ways to build a new life."
—*Jo Parfitt, author of Career in Your Suitcase*

"Robin Pascoe holds a mirror up to the expat soul and shows it for what it is: delighted, resentful, joyful, and miserable, and often all on the same day. The glue that holds every overseas assignment together is the accompanying spouse, and Ms. Pascoe's book is the best how-to guide a girl ever had."
—*Review posted at amazon.com*

"This book covers every topic and makes it all seem doable. I read several books before moving overseas, but none of them really prepared me like this one. Best of all, it was great to laugh while reading about the ups and downs of a major life change."
—*Review posted at amazon.com*

"Robin Pascoe has skilfully and with great humour put her finger on all the issues that arise when moving abroad with your husband. Oh how I wish I had been given this book five years ago when I began this career. I recommend this book for first-timers and veterans alike, we are not alone."
—*Review posted at amazon.com*

"Robin's quick wit and sense of humour are skilfully interwoven within the pages of *A Broad Abroad* along with her unwavering commitment to provide women with the information they need to help them decide if they want to embark on the journey as an expat accompanying spouse."
—*Debra R. Bryson, co-author of* A Portable Identity

"Robin Pascoe brings her distinctive voice—clear, incisive, funny, realistic, and wise—to our understanding of the global family's experience. Reading her book is like walking on the beach with a friend and meeting with an experienced, professional mentor at the same time. Not everyone will have the same ups and downs Robin and her family had, but every expat will benefit from reading her story and mulling over her advice."
—*Anne Copeland, Director, Interchange Institute*

"This is Robin's manifesto for expatriate wives around the world."
—*Rodney Briggs, long-suffering and much-maligned husband of the author*

"With her unique combination of warmth, understanding, humour, and feisty advocacy, Robin Pascoe has become a beloved standard-bearer for women accompanying their partners on overseas assignments. I'm very glad that this honest and supportive book will continue to guide and reassure new generations of expat women. This book was, and is, a landmark contribution to the cause."
—*Patricia Linderman, co-author of* The Expert Expat

"Robin takes all the pus and pain out of the expat experience, mixes in a dose of true compassion and common sense, flavours it with utterly incorrigible humor—then dishes it up as something entirely palatable and ridiculously practical. Delicious."
—*Marie Brice, expat life coach*

To Merle,
Enjoy reading
about my crazy
life!
All the
best
Rol Pascoe

A BROAD ABROAD

Also by Robin Pascoe

Raising Global Nomads:
Parenting Abroad in an On-Demand World

A Moveable Marriage:
Relocate Your Relationship without Breaking It

Homeward Bound:
A Spouse's Guide to Repatriation

Culture Shock! A Parent's Guide

A Broad Abroad

The Expat Wife's Guide to Successful Living Abroad

ROBIN PASCOE

Expatriate Press
Vancouver

Expatriate Press Limited

1430 Terrace Avenue
North Vancouver, BC
Canada V7R 1B4
(604) 990-4532 (tel)
ww.expatexpert.com
robinpascoe@shaw.ca

ISBN: 978-0-9686760-5-9

Copy-edited by Naomi Pauls, Paper Trail Publishing
Cover and text design by Patty Osborne, Vancouver Desktop Publishing
Cover photo taken by Rosy Lara before personally transporting the author to a speaking engagement at the American Women's Club of Amsterdam in a traditional Dutch *bakfiets*.
Author photo by Tamara Roberts

To Rodney, always, with love

Contents

Acknowledgments

In bringing my original book about the challenges of being an expatriate wife back into print, I have received encouragement and assistance from many sources. My family, who are now used to being used so shamelessly to frame my content, of course need to be acknowledged first and foremost for their love and support. I'm grateful for my talented editor Naomi Pauls, book designer Patty Osborne, and web designer Angela Wangsawidjaja for making it all happen. My husband Rodney, to whom this book is dedicated, has encouraged and supported my writing and publishing business for expatriate families from the beginning and deserves a medal for putting up with me. Finally, I want to thanks the tens of thousands of expat wives around the world who, over the past twenty years, have shared with me their experiences and stories, sometimes with brutal, painful honesty. They continue to be my source of inspiration.

Introduction to New Edition

I t is hard to imagine now, with literally hundreds of thousands of words about the experiences and issues of the accompanying partner in print and online, that this was the *first* book to ever challenge the conventional and, in my opinion, extremely convenient wisdom that an international relocation would be easy for a wife. Nothing to think or worry about; just get on with it; all will be well. These were among the platitudes many of us were told—and some of us still hear today—often in a helpful but highly dismissive, irritating, and worse, patronizing tone.

Entitled *Culture Shock! A Wife's Guide* when it first appeared in bookstores in 1992, this book broke a taboo by speaking out publicly about the challenges of the mobile life for the mobile wife (which, incidentally, was one of the book's first working titles). At the time, I just wanted to tell the honest-to-goodness truth about what becoming an accompanying wife really involved, *both* the good and the bad. I felt success would be more assured and decisions to move more informed if women knew what really awaited them.

So many excellent books have since followed: other realistic accounts of expat life as a wife and mother, helpful guides to setting new career goals and keeping one's identity, plus books to help children raised overseas, third culture kids (TCKs). All of these volumes and more have contributed to an excellent body of expat family literature.

At first, no one was remotely interested in publishing *this* book. When I began writing it in 1989, in the brief two-hour reprieve I had every morning when my then toddler son Jay went to a Taipei nursery school, I was considered radical. How dare I say, *"Hold on here,* there's more to this story than just following 'my man.'" The rejection letters I got from publishers were illuminating. The one most revealing of attitudes of the day came from a Hong Kong publisher who wrote: "Expat wives have servants. Why do they need a book?"

Corporations were not pleased with me either. They worried that after reading this particular book, a woman might decide an international move was *not* for her. That could halt plans for an international assignment for one of their employees. Spousal reluctance to relocate remains a huge deal-breaker in global mobility—ironically, for many of the reasons articulated for the first time in this book, most of which were patently obvious. I often remind people that my books are not rocket science. While speaking abroad, I have met many women who confirmed that this book gave them pause before they agreed to move. "Good, I did my job," I would respond to them then as now. "I made you think about what you were getting yourself into. And here you are!"

Seen by some as a radical trying to start a revolution among spouses, I was also, unfortunately, accused by some of being *anti-feminist*. This book was written for women almost exclusively. It excluded men because they handle issues of self-esteem differently, and I knew a good chunk of the content addressed how a woman feels about herself, usually lousy in the early days. The idea of the book being exclusive to women funnily enough did not sit well with feminists back in the politically correct days of the early 1990s when the book first appeared in the United States. The original title assigned by the publisher only added fuel to their ire. It should have been titled, I was informed by irate feminists, *A Spouse's Guide*.

I was living at home in Canada at that time, between Rodney's overseas diplomatic assignments. Overcommitted to the point of burnout and exhaustion, I spent a good part of my time volunteering on the board of directors at a local women's shelter for abused women. Yet, at the same time, I was accused of setting women's issues back twenty years by writing what I did, according to the letters the U.S. publisher received. The hurt and betrayal I felt cut deep (so deep that I began calling myself a "recovering feminist"). Apparently, the other major book distributors (these were pre-Amazon.com days) also felt I was guilty of portraying expat wives as dependents. Never mind that this book is all about getting *over* feeling dependent!

No one actually read beyond the title. It did not help, I suppose, that if someone did make it to the inside pages, they would see that I refused the publisher's instructions to change my suggestion that a woman have a baby abroad to take advantage of help if it was easily available. The tone of this and the four books I have subsequently written for expatriate families (and, indeed, the tone I also take in my lectures) has always been one of irreverence, my tongue pressed firmly in my cheek. Despite the serious nature of these subjects and the importance of telling the truth, using humour and constantly stressing the significant part that comic relief plays in successfully living abroad remains, in my view, the best way I can raise awareness of these important themes that too many women keep hidden. Comedy, I was told once, is tragedy plus time. It is also a great tool for storytelling. My choice to use an irreverent tone was also my own way of fighting back against all the earnest "happy-faced stories" I was being told about life abroad, like how great the shopping would be wherever we were being posted.

I did not need information on the availability of designer purses or shoes (not that there is anything wrong with shopping). Like most women I met, what I *really* wanted to know was whether or not I would be able to cope with all the losses that would be the hallmark of the peripatetic life of an expat. The number of gains one experiences is enormous. However, it is the losses—career, identity, paycheque, friends, relatives, life props, to name just a few—which I needed desperately to understand, so I could manage both my feelings and my expectations. As my mentor, the late Dr. David Pollock, co-author of

Third Culture Kids, the bible about TCKs, used to say: "The positives will take care of themselves. It's the negatives that need to be addressed."

When the first draft of this book was completed, I asked my husband, Rodney, whom you will hear a lot about in these pages, to read it and tell me his thoughts. I will never forget his first critique: "Maybe I should consider a different career!" His comments sprung from my worries that our marriage would not survive all the anger and resentment I was feeling towards him. Naturally, Rodney was blamed constantly for the loss of my self-esteem. That message came out a little too clearly at first. I toned it down significantly and at the same time reminded myself: No one *forced* me to move. I made a choice. It was just not as *informed* a choice as I would have preferred it to have been. When I subsequently met and heard the stories of other women who had similarly jumped into the expat life without a parachute, I decided to make sure those who followed me would know *exactly* what they were getting into so they could make a decision to move based on tangible information.

That is when I discovered no such book had yet been written. We were still in universal denial of the challenges. What was needed, I felt, was an emotional yet practical guide for a married woman who relocates internationally, written by someone who had been there and done that. My training as a journalist would be an asset—it was a career choice I could not pursue in a conventional way without press credentials, withheld from diplomatic spouses in most places where we lived. I would just have to teach myself how to be an author (with a two-year-old son freaked out in Taiwan), but I wanted to unabashedly and unapologetically write a book for women.

Nowadays, when I lecture abroad about repatriation, marriage, and raising global nomads, or even when I speak about work-life balance or other business-related issues to international human resources practitioners, someone comes up to my book table and invariably asks for *this* book. At some

women's club meetings, I can count on a member bringing me
their battered old copy and asking me to sign it, usually telling
me that she has clung to it after lending a previous copy that was
never returned. Or a parent at an international school lecture
comes up with the companion piece I wrote soon after while
living in Beijing. (I wrote it in a mahjong room at a health and
social club we were lucky enough to be able to join.) That book,
called *Culture Shock! A Parent's Guide*, I transformed into a
new, more current book *Raising Global Nomads: Parenting
Abroad in an On-Demand World*, released in 2006. Still another
expat wife may tell me their husband bought this book for them
and they were thankful he did. Sometimes I am handed a book
I signed fifteen years ago! Even my handwriting looks younger.

Clearly women still need and want to read this book, which
got me thinking about getting it back into print. I worried,
though, that expat life had changed so much for the wife as to
make the challenges I had written about earlier irrelevant. Yet,
in travelling from community to community over the past two
decades, I have heard stories from women that prove they are
still struggling with career challenges, loss of their identities,
relationships that need realignments, and, of course, culture
shock during transition.

Families and in particular spouses continue to go out badly
prepared by companies and organizations, and are still carrying
unrealistic expectations. That is why I feel that *do-it-yourself*
expats are still the unsung heroes of this experience and enjoy
hearing their comments when I meet them at schools or clubs.
Because they must do everything on their own, they often
express utter disbelief over what "supported" expats complain
about and in many cases, rightly so. Likewise, families posted to
hardship postings on international development projects to
places far removed from the tourist map, or missionaries who
also live off-road, deserve the respect and admiration of those of
us who moved to cities or countries where a mosquito is just a
mosquito (and does not carry any threat of dengue fever) and

amenities like grocery or department stores are taken for granted.

I hold military families, though, in my highest esteem. They courageously and with tremendous grace take the hardest hits of all because they not only move often, but an absent parent is off serving a country, not a company, putting his or her life in danger not from BlackBerry overload, but from a hostile army. They should inspire all of us.

All women, I have learned over the years, *still* need validation and reassurance that they are not the only one feeling lonely and isolated by this way of living, despite the biggest change to expat life to happen since I started writing books about global living: the Internet!

Technology, the Internet, mobile phones, YouTube, and social media like Twitter, Facebook, and LinkedIn have changed expatriate life dramatically—for the better. In so many ways it has never been easier to be an expat. Accompanying spouses can receive more support (both emotional and practical) than ever before from each other online. Shopping can be done over the Internet; friends and family can remain in touch easily; family blogs can show grandparents what their children and grandchildren are doing; careers can be maintained (or new ones pursued) thanks to the wireless world; and expatriate websites, chat groups, and social media have created online expatriate communities, allowing families to find support and comfort in the knowledge that everyone faces similar challenges no matter where they are in the world. Likewise, a rising number of personal blogs provide a terrific source of both information and inspiration. Need to find toothpicks? Now it is very easy to just ask someone by phone, text, e-mail, chat, and so on.

Yet information delivered over a computer or even in the pages of a book will never replace the human contact spouses desperately need when they first arrive in an unfamiliar place and begin the process of reinventing their lives. In 2008, with the support of my sponsor, the Canadian moving and relocation company AMJ

Campbell International, I conducted and published the results of an extensive relocation survey called Family Matters! (You can read the fascinating—and validating—results at no cost on the home page of my website, www.expatexpert.com.) Topping the list of what families (and wives, who represented the majority of respondents) told me they needed upon arrival was *a human face.* In so many instances, the partner whose job brought them abroad was not there to do the hand-holding.

What is different about this edition? Well, it's not new but it certainly has had a good edit. Women who may have read it almost twenty years ago when it first appeared will suddenly think, *Hey, I've read this book before!* And then, with a laugh I hope, they will realize how different they are now, recognizing how much they have learned about the experience and themselves before giving the book to someone new to the life. Being older now, I have arrived at a great vantage point for reflection and the wisdom that can only come with age.

I have slipped in some changes to the text here and there. Sometimes I have made a reference to the books I wrote afterwards with new lessons to share; in other instances, I have inserted research that I felt was necessary to add. This new introduction is obviously designed to bring the original readers up to date. And I have expanded the Resources to lead women to my favourite books and websites. But as I said at the outset, there is just so much excellent material out there now that I could not possibly list all of it.

In releasing this updated and revised edition, I am hoping that new readers, as they did before, will feel less alone when reading it. They will be reassured in reading my stories—and those of other women—that are so similar to their own. They will have their own feelings made real.

As I suggest to women when lecturing about my book *A Moveable Marriage,* leave a copy of *A Broad Abroad* on your husband's side of the bed. Rodney told other husbands in a group gathered in Beijing to hear me speak soon after its original publication that it makes "great defensive reading" for guys. He has never heard me lecture since that one time. That is probably a good thing, since I use him shamelessly to get a laugh. I have certainly made him read all of my books very carefully though, and not just to help me find any typos!

Finally, it is my belief that no one knows the expat experience better than someone who has lived it; no one is better equipped to help a new expat wife than another one. So remember that the next time a new spouse arrives in your community looking shell-shocked. That used to be you.

Introduction
Exotic Ruts

It is easy to picture her standing at a cocktail party in some distant land, respectably dressed, sipping from a glass, and smiling at some foreign official with whom she is engaged in polite conversation. More likely, the image you have of her is from a television newscast, where she steps off an emergency evacuation flight in the middle of the night, baby in one arm and toddler clinging to the other, looking like she just came through a war (which she may well have done).

Who is she? She is the international travelling wife. Instead of moving to the next street, state, or province, she relocates every few years from one side of the world to another. Married to someone in a foreign service, enlisted in the armed forces, or working for a multinational corporation or organization, a bank, a news bureau, a church, or merely a small export business, she is the ultimate portable wife and probably a mother too. Her career is mobile, her makeup duty-free. She can say "please" and "thank you" in several languages and knows how to evaluate a school or household help in thirty seconds. In the wake of her husband's career, she and her husband and children seem to effortlessly glide from one exotic outpost to another. She is also the last person anybody really thinks about until all the clean underwear runs out.

Behind that friendly facade of competence and sociability there often lurks one very scared, emotionally exhausted, and in many cases angry and resentful "accompanying" wife. On good days, she can easily extol the virtues of an overseas assignment, not the least of which is the romance and adventure of life in a foreign culture. She can watch as her children grow up in an international setting, offering them a "liberal arts childhood" by enlarging their world with culture and travel.

But talk to her on a bad day, perhaps while she seems to be sipping demurely from that drink at a reception, and you will discover that she is in fact irritated beyond words to have been forced to attend her third cocktail party of the week, only to engage in the same pointless small talk she has made thousands of times before in other countries to officials who could not care less about her other than that she is Mrs. Husband's Job.

"And how are you enjoying our country?" the official asks her wherever she is in the world.

"I'm so glad we moved here," she will lie. "The people are so warm and friendly that I just love it here already," she'll say, drinking quickly so as not to choke on her own hypocrisy. On that day, it may just so happen, far from being caught up in the romance of a new assignment, she is in the throes of the hostility common to the early adjustment period. Instead of warm and friendly, she has found the locals intrusive, rude, and stupid. She wants to go home.

"It's been so easy settling in," she may continue, all the while remembering the ancient dirt and grime that coated her apartment walls and the countless phone calls to non-existent numbers in a futile search for good domestic help or a grocery that operates a delivery service.

"I am so happy to hear that," the official will lie back to her. *These foreign women have it so good,* he thinks. *Rich bitches.*

His own transparent resentment will likely go unnoticed. She is too busy thinking how she struggled through an hour's worth of congested traffic just to stand there drinking on an empty stomach while back at her apartment or house, her children are probably working over the new babysitter, who keeps giving in to their every whim despite her clear instructions.

At the other side of the room stands the angst-ridden neophyte to expatriate life, the one who wonders how a woman like herself from a small town ended up clutching a sweaty glass, her third one, mind you, in the past twenty minutes, because some wandering waiter keeps zeroing in on her, forcing her to drink more than she knows she should.

Am I dressed properly? she asks herself for the thousandth time. *Why don't I look as relaxed as the woman standing over there with that foreign official? Oh no, he's coming over here now.* She gulps.

"And how are you enjoying our country?" she is asked.

"Excuse me?"

"How are you enjoying our country?"

"I'm terribly sorry, but I can't seem to understand what you are saying."

Is he speaking English?

"HOW . . . ARE . . . YOU . . . LIKING . . . MY . . . COUNTRY?" he says, wondering how soon he can go home to his own wife, who is not always invited—and perhaps just as well—to these functions.

"Oh, of course, your COUNTRY. It's very nice. The people are so nice, too. It's so nice to be here." *Help me,* she screams.

She glances over to another wife engaged in a heated discussion with a pinstriped man.

"So why can't I work here?" she overhears the woman saying.

"You can work here."

"I'm not a secretary and I don't want to stamp visas. I'm a journalist and I want to work as one. Is that so unreasonable?" she is demanding to know.

"I've told you many times, dear. That one's not up to me," a man, obviously her husband, replies wearily.

"Then why don't I ask *him?*" she says, pointing to the official. *There, that ought to wipe the patronizing grin off your face,* she thinks.

"Please don't do that, dear," he warns, trying to ward off a diplomatic incident.

"And how do you like our country?"

I'd like it a lot better if you let me work here, the former career woman is thinking but instead holds her smile as tightly as her glass and says: "Oh, it's just lovely here. Excuse me, please. I'll leave you men alone to chat."

Stupid cow, thinks the official. *She won't even talk to me.*

Today's expat wife could be any one of those women or all of them at the same time. She willingly (more or less) agreed to follow her husband on his overseas assignment because the thought of foreign adventure seemed intriguing when explained to her around her kitchen table back home. Hearing about all those opportunities to travel, the allure of different domestic set-ups, cost-of-living allowances to compensate for her having to drop out of the workforce—in short, a golden neo-colonial lifestyle—sounded exotic as could be and an escape from the rut she had clearly dug herself into at home.

Instead, here she is in a new routine, with a different backdrop that certainly is exotic, but is also so confusing and alien she cannot even figure out where to buy toothpicks.

Her children are taken care of and she does not know how on earth to fill her time, especially if the local authorities will not let her work at her own profession or, in some countries, even volunteer locally. Worse still, she is expected to learn to play bridge, tennis, and golf; speak the local language fluently and find a dressmaker to create a local sensation for her to wear to a fancy dress ball in three week's time.

She is an emotional mess and this might not even be her first time overseas. *Why wasn't it like this last time?* she may wonder. *Oh, right. I didn't have kids then; or I was pregnant; or my children were still babies; or my husband was still in a junior position and I saw him more, and on and on.*

Even if you have never personally met any of these travelling wives, you have likely heard of a friend who has a friend who every few years sets off for yet another foreign posting. Her stories, even heard second-hand, always sound thrilling. There is no lack of stimulation in her life.

True enough. But there is also more to this story than meets the eye. If you are about to become an accompanying partner yourself, or are considering it and cannot decide whether the idea excites you or depresses you, there are a few things you need to know in order to make an informed decision about going. Chances are you will swim like the best of them within months, but it is worth knowing a few things ahead of time so that an unexpected reef or rock does not bonk you on the head. For those women repeating the experience, you may want to reacquaint yourself with the emotional hurdles you have to negotiate yet again before you regain your equilibrium.

I hope you will find at least some of the advice contained within these pages useful. Too many women are moving overseas with little preparation to help them manage their often inflated and totally unrealistic expectations. Worse, they rarely have anyone to guide them through the emotional transition from life at home to life abroad. A healthy state of mind is critical if an accompanying wife is to fashion a new life that is a satisfying and rewarding experience for her as well as for her family.

It is not enough to simply learn the practicalities of renting a house, shipping a dog with the lampshades, or finding new schools for the children. A woman needs reassurance that she is not losing her mind because she is anxious about day-to-day life in a new culture. She needs to know that it is totally normal to feel exhausted in the first few months and that other newly arrived women also want to do nothing but sit around and watch DVDs, text friends back home, drink a Starbucks latte where it is possible, or just read trashy escapist novels all day instead of joining a club or meeting new people.

She especially needs to know that on some days it is all right to feel like she cannot stand herself, cannot face her own image in the mirror, hates her hair, her body, and most of all her husband for dragging her halfway around the world to watch her own self-esteem plummet, her sense of identity vanish in the new time zone, and her self-confidence get thrown away with the empty moving boxes. She is not the first woman, nor will she be the last, to watch her emotions do battle while her sense of self-worth gets up and walks away.

Most important of all, she needs to know that life *does* return to normal, and that after experiencing the ultimate crisis of confidence, she will become—and feel like—herself again. Only there will be much *more* to her. A woman simply cannot move around the world, live in a different culture, adapt, raise her children, make new friends, and travel without becoming a more fascinating person, with experiences that contribute to opinions and stories worth listening to. She simply will never be the same again.

Why am I qualified to hand out advice on this subject? Over a fifteen-year period in the final two decades of the last century, I was fortunate to experience life from expatriate to repatriate, beginning with our first overseas assignment to Bangkok, where my husband worked for the Canadian Embassy. The Thai capital was followed by postings to Taipei, Beijing, and Seoul, with re-entries to Foreign Affairs headquarters in Ottawa, Canada, in between, and a final move outside of the foreign service to Vancouver, British Columbia, where I hope to never see another moving box and so far, so good.

Since we repatriated, I have spent another dozen years writing and publishing three more books for expat families, writing numerous articles, conducting surveys, and travelling to more than two dozen countries—and almost an equal number of capital cities—meeting members of expat communities first-hand in the process of delivering lectures on the topics of my books. Through my popular website ExpatExpert.com, which has been on the Internet for over a decade now, I have also made myself readily available online to any expat spouse with questions or who is just having a bad day.

Another important bona fide of mine is having had the "first baby born overseas" experience, which, for many expat wives, can be a rite of passage. Our daughter Lilly was born in a Bangkok hospital operating room by Caesarian section. I was attended by an oversupply of nurses, who seemed like midgets compared to the nine pound two ounce girl who was mercifully removed from me in a surreal birthing sequence I doubt Franz Kafka could describe. My pregnancy was a miserable experience, compounded by the worst case of culture shock, since my daughter arrived nine months and two weeks after my husband and I did. Nobody advised me that it might be wise to wait a few months to allow myself to make the countless adjustments to a new life overseas. In fact, nobody advised me of much of anything, which is why I decided in the first place to write this book.

What makes a successful expat wife? More than anything else, it is the ability to keep laughing, even when you want to lock the bathroom door and not come out until the assignment is over. If you do lock yourself in, though, please take this book along with you. It will ensure your sense of humour does not get lost in transition.

1 Pre-Moving Day Jitters
Due to Circumstances Beyond Your Control

Just weeks before our departure to Taiwan for my husband's second overseas assignment, all hell broke loose in Beijing's Tiananmen Square. The Chinese government, which was thought to be encouraging a more enlightened political era, chose instead to open fire on democracy and killed many of the young people who had been demonstrating for such an ideal. China plunged backwards into repression and martial law.

That image may be hard to reconcile in 2009, twenty years later, especially with more recent TV images of a modern Beijing playing host to the 2008 Summer Olympics. Back in 1989, however, the unexpected bloodshed in the Chinese capital became a worldwide media event. Hyped-up news specials screamed from the television screens. The story took up entire newscasts (a precursor to 24-hour news channels), with content that raised everyone's anxiety levels by about two notches within minutes. Elaborate video graphics flashed out the message *China in crisis!* They might just as well have screamed to me personally *Do not go there!*

Overnight, everyone was a China expert. Rarely was the prognosis optimistic, even from the genuine Sinophiles, at least not in the short term. It was this short term that particularly concerned me. My husband Rodney's job as a foreign service officer was taking us and our two young children, our then two-year-old son Jay and six-year-old daughter Lilly, first to Taiwan for one year of Mandarin language training. Following that, we would take up residence in Beijing for a two-year assignment. By my calculations at the time, the short-term period everybody was so pessimistic about would roughly cover the years we would spend living on mainland China.

As if my pre-departure anxiety over the situation in Asia was not bad enough, it was then further fuelled by television coverage of an equally graphic news event that coincided with the China turmoil. From Iran came horrifying footage of the funeral of the Ayatollah Khomeini. The world watched as millions of distraught Iranian men banged their fists against their heads in a show of mourning. Mobbing their spiritual leader's coffin, they forced it to open and the body lying within it to fall to the ground.

"Sorry, dear, but I'm not moving anywhere," I informed my husband as we shut off the television after another particularly unnerving newscast. "The world is too fluid. It's a mess."

"Relax," said my husband knowledgeably, the quintessential unflappable diplomat. "The world's always been a mess. We can just watch the mess now on television, especially in China. There's been far worse going on there. Nothing's different."

"Far worse? You really know how to reassure a woman."

"You know what I mean. You're a big girl. You've travelled a lot."

"I don't want to be a big girl! There's no way I'm taking my children out into that big bad world, especially to Asia. You can go on this assignment alone." Of course, I ended up going. I am neither cool nor unflappable, and together we are living proof of the attraction of opposites. I fell in love with a man who fell in love with travelling around the world. I *chose* to become a travelling wife.

Life Can Be Dangerous at Home

An international crisis is not the greatest prelude to a foreign assignment, especially if it is in the country you are headed for. But despite what appears daily in the news, it has never been a safer time to be an expat. Remember that so many used to die of malaria and other diseases or even just in shipwrecks getting to their posting. The statistical probability for a ruptured appendix in the middle of nowhere was far higher than being caught in the crossfire of terrorism. It is wise to bear in mind that you can encounter danger anywhere. You do not have to travel to find it. When I was living as an expat, I had a better chance statistically of dying in a highway accident back home in Canada.

It is also true that some people thrive on danger, so to them, a world crisis or disaster makes for more adventurous travel and lots of tales for their blogs. They enjoy the shock value of informing friends they are off to a war zone. However, the majority of people, wives and especially mothers, do not particularly want danger included in the package. As a former television news reporter, though, I have always been aware that news reports, while they may be technically accurate, do not always tell the entire truth. Things often look worse from a distance. It is a fact of expatriate life that as a short-term resident of a foreign country, you will likely be unaffected by internal events.

Still, the threat of danger should not be part of the package, and in my own case, I certainly reminded my husband of this fact, probably too much for his liking. I could not help voicing my worries over and over again. The danger element of travelling, not the exotic lifestyle that lay ahead, was prominent in my thoughts, my dreams, my nightmares, indeed my everyday consciousness.

Hiding Your Fears

If you are afraid of going overseas, do not be ashamed to admit it. I believe the days of solid-like-a-brick colonial wives have vanished along with colonialism. The rules have changed: you are allowed to let your emotions surface. Go ahead, be real.

Being an emotional type myself, I am incapable of acting blasé about danger. I will continue in the face of it if I have to, but my eyes will always give away my terror. When my children were little and I did not want to transfer my fears onto them, I could have won an Academy Award for "best performance by a mother concealing her fear." Take the time I had to fly home from our first posting in Bangkok with my then two-year-old daughter Lilly. It was only one week after an Air India plane originating in Canada had been blown out of the sky. Only a robot could have boarded a flight bound for Canada looking unafraid of potential terrorism. But I became a robot after confessing my deepest, darkest fears only to my husband (who naturally had a few fears of his own about sending his wife and daughter off at a time of aviation piracy). My daughter would never have guessed I was afraid, unless she was suspicious of the numerous fancy glasses filled with heavy splashes of a rich alcoholic substance known as brandy that the flight attendant fortunately brought me like clockwork once we were airborne. In truth, I was not sure what scared me more: the threat of a terrorist attack, twenty-four hours in the air with a toddler, or my profound fear of flying, even on a bright clear day.

Talking about your fears may not prevent them from materializing. Internalizing them, however, will be another source of stress you can do without.

Preparing Your Children

When our second Asian assignment grew nearer, and televised history was unfolding in Beijing, I recognized that six-year-old Lilly needed to be briefed about the situation in China. I was worried that her kindergarten school chums might frighten her by repeating what they had heard their parents say about China. Of course, informing a little girl about the politics of China may sound a bit far-fetched, but it was not completely impossible. I just told her that the Chinese people were a little upset and wondering about their future, not unlike the way she was wondering what it would be like to move away. I also asked her if anyone had mentioned anything to her about China. She thought my question over for a minute. "You know, Mom," she said, looking perplexed, "nobody really cares that I'm moving. Why is that?"

"Well . . . ," I began. *Beats me,* I thought. It is almost easier to explain calamities or foreign politics to your children than it is to help them understand their friends' indifferent attitudes towards their pending move. Inadvertently, she was getting her first experience of the way non-travelling families view those who do. "It's kind of an early lesson in life," I answered, only adding to her confusion. She had time enough to learn that as an adult, she would receive similar apathetic reactions from friends when the subject of life abroad came up.

Instead of politics, it is better to concentrate on your children's emotional well-being by watching for signs of depression or unhappiness, such as sullenness or lack of appetite. Like adults, information is the key to children's readiness for life overseas, and it could help them get over any moodiness. Whatever facts you learn through your pre-departure briefings, books, or on the Internet, share them with your children. Help them find out what they are most interested in knowing by doing a web search on the country you are headed for. Connect them though Facebook with someone else at the school they will attend.

For younger children, the information you hand out will be slightly different. One of the best reassurances I could give my fearful six-year-old daughter before she would start grade one in Taipei was the news that just about everyone in her class would also likely be new and not know anybody else.

It also helps children get used to the idea of a move if you let them help with the preparations as much as possible. Give children of all ages a list of things they can do, like sorting out their toys or clothes. Do not exclude them from packing up. Older children are feeling alienated enough from their friends, so try not to make them feel like outsiders at home. Younger children want to be part of the action too. Continually point out the bonuses of moving abroad, such as more exotic holidays that you will be able to take as a family. While you are at it, convince *yourself* of these bonuses.

Something to keep in mind, though: your children only remember when things go wrong. A smooth move is forgettable. Perhaps you, like us, arrive at a posting with a bald dog, as we did in Seoul, Korea. We had decided to take our Shetland sheepdog with us on that posting, only to lose him in the airport for hours upon arrival. When we finally found him, he was hairless from the stress of the long flight. I can assure you that as a family, you will be sharing and laughing over these kinds of stories years later.

Emotional Roller Coaster

In the pre-departure stage, a woman's mood can change several times a day. Before our second time moving abroad, no sooner had I got over my immediate hysteria about events in China than my mood shifted from fear to shame: what kind of person was I to personalize the trauma of the Chinese people? Was I that shallow and superficial to be so worried about the availability of Cheerios when the fate of a billion people hung in the balance? Horrified that I could be so self-absorbed, I struggled to regain perspective.

In the end, I managed to convince myself that as a mother and foreign service wife, my feelings were running wild for very legitimate reasons. All of my life props were being taken away as our family headed for the great unknown to become, once again, an unknown quantity. This was not my first time moving abroad, but now I was a parent, which made a huge difference.

Of course I was concerned about the future of China. But I was about to travel to Beijing by myself after a home leave in Canada, alone with my two young children because my husband had gone ahead. I will be perfectly honest about what was uppermost in my mind. It was not aging Chinese leaders. It was surviving the journey!

Before I left Canada for Beijing, a good friend took me to lunch and queried my recent weight loss.

"Deep stress burns calories."

"Worried about China?" she naturally asked.

"Sure," I replied, "right after I get through worrying about how to put together our hardship shipment of two hundred rolls of toilet paper, find room in our luggage for all the clothes and toys my family has given the children while we've been home, haul all that luggage through Vancouver and Hong Kong airports by myself with the kids, survive the twenty-four hours of flying from here to Beijing without killing myself or them . . . Should I go on?" I asked. Naturally I had not touched the food sitting in front of me.

"So aren't you scared?"

"I'm scared of so many things happening to us that it's all evened out. I'm numb."

Wild mood swings from euphoria to feelings of total despair are among the signs that time is running out and moving day is fast approaching. Excitement about the prospect of a new foreign culture is quickly replaced with the anxiety of dealing with the endless details that must be attended to before you can get on the plane. The relief you initially felt with the thought of getting away from the often petty hassles of family can turn to sadness that you will be missing your father's seventieth birthday. Even the thought of leaving behind your dog can bring a lump to your throat.

You may not be feeling your best either. Unlike the deep stress before my third departure that forced me to alter my clothes, the reverse had happened before we left for the second time. Then, we embarked upon an Endless Farewell Dinner Party, which lasted about two months and added at least five pounds to my waist from too much eating and drinking. My sleep was erratic, and I would awaken long before dawn to mentally add to my to-do list for that day. To cope with all my moves and keep my emotions and practical details separate, I resorted to a child's notebook, divided into two simple sections: Things to Do; Things to Buy. I felt in control of something, even if it was only errands.

Feelings of complete distraction and an inability to focus your thoughts are also completely natural side effects of the anxiety you are feeling. So find something—a book, exercise program, whatever—to give you a temporary escape from all those details. I was so distracted before our second move that I started watching movies in the afternoon. I even holed up in a darkened movie theatre to watch the original Batman movie twice in three days. I told my husband it was because I needed a good dose of North American pop culture to keep me going for three years. I was desperate for diversions and settled on a dark knight.

There is simply no way around feeling stressed out. It's *pre-departure culture shock* and no one is exempt, no matter how many times you have moved before. Each move is different (like pregnancies) because the stage of your life, the age of your children, and other human factors will have changed since the last time. If it *is* your first time out, do not dismiss your overwhelming fear of the unknown. It will colour everything.

Physically you have not left home, but emotionally you are beginning to feel alienated from your friends and family, who just do not understand what you are going through. How could they unless they have moved abroad themselves? I knew I had reached my stress threshold when I desperately wanted to smoke a cigarette after giving them up eleven years earlier. (I will not go into the expatriate "going back to smoking after quitting for years" phenomenon other than to say I have never tried to quit smoking again so many times in my life.) The pre-departure stress can be for so many different reasons, it is impossible to pinpoint the exact cause. There are the details of selecting a moving company, the nightmare of preparing an inventory of your belongings, the sadness of closing down your residence, shutting off life in one country to be turned on in the next one. Fear can also feed your stress.

Marital relations are likely not peaking either. On a good day, you think your husband is wonderful for giving you such a fabulous adventure. On a bad day, like the day you have to clean out your garage or basement for your new tenant, you will want to kill him for getting you into it. (I deal with resentment and anger in chapter 9.)

Coping with Disaster Syndrome

When I first confessed to a friend that I had a horrible fear of losing everyone dear to me overnight, usually by fiery car accident or plane disaster, I was relieved to hear my friend tell me she suffered from the same secret paranoia. Soon after, I discovered that what I was privately calling *disaster syndrome,* imagining the worst possible scenarios for loved ones, was the so-called mature woman's replacement for anorexia nervosa. It seemed that all around me, other women were also imagining themselves as widows, childless, and loveless. Now, in this new century, we live in the age of anxiety where "fear of the unknown," almost a kissing cousin to disaster syndrome, has actually been labelled *pre-traumatic stress syndrome* (worrying about something that *might* happen).

This sense of pending doom is heightened when you are about to move abroad, especially if world events run amok and you are watching, listening, or reading about them 24/7. The familiar, safe environment of home is about to be removed, and so many new factors over which you have no control enter into the picture.

Never mind world events if your children are teenagers, as you will likely be worried about what trouble they could get into overseas. If they stay behind for college or boarding school, you will still be worried that they are out of your sphere of influence. And what about your marriage? Everyone wonders how their marriage will survive the tensions of life abroad, where you can feel literally glued to your spouse financially and emotionally. That is why I wrote *A Moveable Marriage: Relocate Your Relationship without Breaking It.*

And then there is all that flying to get through. As I mentioned, I am desperately afraid of flying, a condition I know I share with thousands of other mothers, even if they have not come right out and confessed to it. Unfortunately, you often cannot avoid flying if you are moving abroad.

On our first posting, my husband and I were still at the stage where whimsy did not have to be scheduled, and as a surprise present before we left, he bought me an antique flask that we dubbed my "flying flask." I filled it with brandy and would smugly board any aircraft knowing that no matter when the drinks cart began its service on board, I could have a good, necessary shot right when I needed it—when the plane rolled down the runway for takeoff.

Our second time out, this time with children, I could no longer afford such open indulgence. For one thing, I could not let my children see their mother sneaking a fearful shot (or two or four), and for another, I needed my wits about me to be able to take my son to the toilet and not drop him. The time had come to do something about my neurotic fear of flying. I had quit smoking with the help of a hypnotist, so I returned for a fear of flying session. As I was going to be in a trance anyway, I asked the hypnotist what post-hypnotic suggestions he could leave with me to help my attitude towards moving, my stress, my inability to learn a foreign language (could I possibly learn Chinese through hypnosis?), and anything else applicable. This more or less worked (although I could not learn Chinese). Now, of course, when even water is treated suspiciously at airport security, the idea of taking carry-on alcohol is a non-starter *and* as my children have grown up (more or less), I am less fearful. Or, perhaps like so many fears we may have when we are younger, with age I have simply gotten over my fear of flying.

There's Not Enough Time!

I am not sure who can ultimately be blamed for this particular phenomenon (since nobody will take responsibility), but a move abroad seems always to be announced at the last minute. I do not mean the principle of an international move. You may hear about the idea for months from your husband, whose boss may have mentioned it a few times, or it may come through equally circuitous routes. My favourite story is a wife who learned she was moving when the moving company called and asked if they could come over to do an estimate! If your husband is a diplomat, like mine was, you know in theory that a move is always possible at any time. The question about a pending move is always twofold: Where are we going? And when will we know for certain?

No matter when the news is finally confirmed, the wife's mind is instantaneously thrown into overdrive. There are a million and one things to get organized, and you cannot possibly do it all in the time allotted.

If there are teenage children involved, your preparations could be further weighted down by a constant refrain of "You're ruining my life!"—hardly helping to inspire the mental energy you need to get the family into planning the move. Besides which, you may want to turn to that teenager and cry "What about *my* life?" but your so-called maturity stops you.

When we moved to Bangkok for our first assignment, it was only at the last minute that Thailand was even confirmed as our destination. I had been working on the assumption that we were moving to Jakarta and was busy extolling the virtues of Java to myself and telling people I would send "care" packages of batik if they were nice to me. Six weeks before we were to move, the location was changed, and my head did a somersault trying to sort out the differences between Thailand and Indonesia, which are considerable.

Know Where You Are Going

Between the stress and the fear, it is easy to overlook that you are about to move to a brand new country you may barely be capable of locating on a map. As a first step, enter the name of the new country into Google. Once upon a time, you could buy an atlas, and you still can, of course, but the Internet is both atlas and encyclopedia rolled into one and should provide lots of information aimed at children of all ages.

The best bet, though, remains a human one: find some people who have lived or travelled where you are going. Information will not only be plentiful in the areas you may be interested in, like moving as a family, but it will be given to you in a personalized way, which is much easier to absorb than dry trade or weather statistics.

Do not be shy about calling up people you have never met, but whose names you have been given. You will quickly learn that the international community, both at home and abroad, is much more receptive to a stranger's phone calls seeking information. Everyone who moves overseas has been in a similar situation at some point in their moving lives. If you are invited over for a drink or dinner, be sure to accept. Social meetings are as useful as formal briefings. It is also a good idea to begin getting used to meeting new people, as this will definitely be part of your life abroad.

Educate Yourself About Schools

Information-gathering about schools should follow the same path as researching the country itself. Talk to others who have been to where you are going and to the professionals who may be overseeing your posting. If that does not prove satisfactory, call the school directly. A few dollars in long-distance charges will be worth the peace of mind. In the resources section of this book, I have provided some links to professional companies that have sprung up in the past decade or so that do nothing but help you find the right school for your children.

Sometimes, general advice can prove useful even if it may not apply to your situation. For instance, before we moved the second time, I heard from other mothers that skills such as reading and writing were often far more advanced in some international schools than what we were used to at home at a similar grade level. Since moving was going to be traumatic enough, I did not want any further surprises for my daughter on the first day of school. Well in advance, we ordered a special series of books that would help her teach herself to read. Take no chances. To be forewarned is to be forearmed.

Deciding What to Take

When we were packing up our home, I followed a general rule of thumb that someone taught me early on in the game: I would never take anything precious overseas. Whether it was a baby picture, a family heirloom, or a favourite book, I would ask myself if I would be distraught if it were lost or broken. If the answer was yes, into storage it went. If you must take something irreplaceable, put it in your purse and carry it on the flight. Similarly, carry on any important documents like birth or health certificates, school records, marriage licenses, and a copy of your wills.

If your children are young, try to pack up their rooms in their entirety, right down to the last stuffed animal. I wish it had been possible to physically transport my children's bedrooms right on the plane, because that would have saved a lot of grief in the period we waited to be resettled.

It is hard deciding just how many sundry items you should load up your shipment with. Often you will hear that certain items are unavailable where you are going and then find out this is not the case once you arrive. (We took so much toothpaste to Bangkok, we actually returned home with some three years later.) Take along anything you feel you cannot live without, like your special brand of makeup or your children's favourite treats. In the age of the Internet, and with most formerly developing countries now offering shopping malls the size of a Western-style suburb, you can pretty much find everything and, if you cannot, order it online.

Saying Goodbye

I already mentioned our own Endless Farewell Dinner Party, which was enjoyable at the time but cumulatively fattening. The reason we partied on so many different occasions was so that we could bypass a big blowout where everyone could come. There is little time to talk with anyone at a huge get-together. Smaller parties, with specific guest lists, seemed like a good solution, but can be high in calorie count. We also seemed to be out all the time and our children wondered quite rightly if their parents had left the country before them. My advice is this: try eating before you go out so you are not as hungry. When that does not work, arrange to get some exercise.

Your children's farewells should be equally as thought-out. You might consider talking with the school about having a cake or small party during school hours. Pay special attention to planning parties for teenage children, who may be especially reluctant to leave their friends.

Try to hold something before everyone disappears for the long school holidays. We chose Canada Day for a children's party before we left the second time. It served the secondary purpose of reminding the children of their nationality, and it was early enough in our summer that people were still around. Saying goodbye to parents, especially if they are getting on in their years, is not as easy to plan. They are usually torn between their emotions: they are happy you are leading an adventurous life, but sorry the grandchildren will be so far away. If they are not well, you will feel the added guilt that you are burdening your siblings with heavier filial responsibilities. Short of cancelling your posting, there is nothing you can do to get around leaving unhappy parents, so plan to bring your children closer to them through the magic of technology.

Meeting the Boss and His Wife

The major goodbye blowout will be with your friends. But before you leave you will also likely have an informal meeting, lunch, or dinner with your husband's boss and his wife (if he is married). Make no mistake: they are checking you out to see how you will represent the company, the government, the product, whatever it is, in a foreign setting.

Most women breeze through this preliminary inspection with flying colours, mostly because they are still on home territory and have not gone into deep culture shock yet at the other end. (I will discuss post-arrival meetings with the boss and his wife at your post in another chapter.) Do not worry about this preliminary inspection. You are still excited, after all, even if a little frazzled by all the preparations, but your enthusiasm should see you through.

I learned the hard way to keep my mouth shut during these pre-tour inspections. Mostly I learned to sublimate my own ego altogether and was able to give no indication (that is, if I was even asked) that I enjoyed a long-standing career of my own as a journalist.

If you feel you may come across as some threatening type who is going to be a headache for the boss, the ambassador, or whoever is in charge by demanding better work opportunities, allow me to suggest this: think very carefully about opening your mouth to offer what may be perceived as strong opinions. Overseas, typecasting of wives as strident troublemakers can be instantaneous and long-lasting. Take it from someone who knows this from personal experience!

Wills, Work, and Financial Affairs

Everyone hates to think of something happening, but do not leave home without making sure your personal affairs are in order. Not only should you make sure you and your husband have made out your wills, but guardians must be appointed for your children in the unlikely event of an accident. It is horrible to contemplate, but it has to be done, so see your lawyer before you leave the country. This will sound even worse, but make sure your wills cover the possibility that your entire family has an accident.

Financial matters overseas can be one of the biggest headaches you can face, although obviously online banking and investing has helped enormously. Still, hire a professional to oversee your affairs while you are away if you can. If you have not already engaged a professional property manager to look after your house, if you own one, make sure you do. Never rely on family and friends to see to your affairs. They lead busy lives and may not get around to *your* affairs as quickly as you would like. However, there may be occasions when you need to appoint someone (usually a sibling or close friend) to hold power of attorney so that they will have the authority to sign official documents on your behalf. This is especially important with regard to buying, selling, or renting property.

Mobile careers and working from overseas is a subject that must be handled separately (see chapter 5, "Careers Can Travel Too"), but in the context of your pre-departure nervousness, my advice is to put work on the back burner. Your state of panic can only get worse if you start worrying about working too. Give yourself a few months to let the dust settle.

Travelling with Children

I have saved this category for last because if your children are young, these will likely be the most elaborate measures you will take, comparable to the battle plans of a general. I delve deeper into some of these challenges in *Raising Global Nomads: Parenting Abroad in an On-Demand World*, but here are a few highlights.

Some airplane strategies

Booking tickets well in advance is always wise, but if you are travelling with children, make sure you pre-book your seats too. These seat assignments should appear on your confirmation computer printout. If you have young movie buffs with you and it is going to be a long-haul flight, check to make sure your aircraft has individual screens. If it does not, consider a portable DVD player to keep the kids amused.

When you tag your hand luggage, make sure you tag your children (yes, you read that right) and everything they are carrying. Put down your name as well and the airline you are travelling on. It does not hurt to add the name of the hotel you will be staying in upon arrival. For some reason, a rumour circulated that bulkhead seats of an airplane are better with small children. While it is true there may be room to put up a cot for a baby, bulkhead seats are otherwise a nightmare of logistics and should be avoided at all costs.

For one thing, all your hand luggage will have to be stowed above you and will be inaccessible during takeoffs and landings. Tables for games, colouring, and eating often have to be brought or attached and will require assistance from members of the flight crew, who may mysteriously disappear for long stretches of time.

A good seating strategy that works if you have two children is this: divide and conquer. Rather than sit four across, where siblings can torture one another, split up into two and two, one behind the other. This way each adult can take on a child individually, and if they go to sleep, it might even be possible for you and your spouse to catch a few minutes of sleep or conversation (but don't count on this).

Mealtime need not be a struggle to get airline mystery meat down your children's throats. It is possible to order a child's special meal from most airlines in advance. All this requires is a request and a reminder when you check in for your flights. Children's meals on some airlines are often better than the regular fare. I devoured my daughter's fresh salad and apple on one flight instead of the usual whipped Jell-O delight offered to the adults. A child's meal is often a hamburger and chips, which can be a reassuring sight for a youngster. Most airlines also serve the children's meals first, which can be very useful when your child is ravenous or cranky.

But just in case all goes awry with your pre-ordering, always travel with your own emergency food kit: small snacks or raisins, granola bar, miniature cereal boxes, or fruit. Especially bring food if you are travelling a no-frills airline. You do not want to see what passes as a snack on some airlines. Remember to buy your carry-on liquids for your children *after* you go through security.

Try to avoid sugary snacks if you want your child to sleep later. However, one sugary treat that is a must for takeoff is a bag of sweets or suckers. Not only will the sucking and swallowing help with the pressure in their ears, but it works like a pacifier. If you are travelling with a baby and worried about the takeoff, begin feeding either by breast or bottle as soon as the pilot begins his roll down the runway.

In-flight crews that are sympathetic to parents are the luck of the draw. Similarly, fellow passengers who do not feel children should be banned from all commercial flights or thrown into the overhead bins will also be decided by fate.

The other passengers are beyond your jurisdiction, but the flight crew is supposed to be there for you. Do not worry about asking them to heat up a bottle or helping yourself to an extra soda water when your child has been sick. On board a long-distance flight, be pushy. If you do not ask, sometimes you just will not receive, and you only hurt yourself by not standing up for the services you have paid for.

Airsickness, and that could be your own as well as your child's, is something that has to be endured. You can help your children and yourself avoid nausea by eating only light, bland foods the day you are travelling. Loading your children's stomachs (or your own, for that matter) with gooey, sweet, even spicy food may not help you when your plane starts bouncing all over the sky in turbulence. Anti-nausea travel medication for adults and children is normally available at drugstores under different brand names depending on where you come from and should be taken before the flight, especially if you have a predisposition to airsickness.

If all the best-laid plans still produce a revolt of the stomach, do not eat anything other than a dry piece of bread or cracker, washed down with ginger ale that has gone flat (or which you have taken the air bubbles out of by stirring with a swizzle-stick). If there is continued throwing-up, make sure you keep drinking fluids. Dehydration from vomiting is bad at the best of times, but up in the sky, breathing air as dry as the Sahara Desert can really dry you out.

One final tip on airplanes: if you are taking a long-distance flight with toddlers, try to book a night flight if one is available. This strategy worked miracles in our family. We took a holiday from Taiwan to Britain and to Spain. Both of the long-haul flights between Hong Kong and London and returning (a mere seventeen hours in the air) began relatively late at night. This meant we could keep our then toddler son Jay up until flight time, put him in his pyjamas as soon as we boarded, bring out his own pillow case for the airplane pillow, and he was asleep before the plane left the runway.

What you pack is what you carry

A travel article about packing once appeared in the *New York Times*, and I have personally followed its advice ever since. It suggested that when you pack, you should first put everything out on your bed that you think you will need. Then, the article advised, you should eliminate half of it. Take a break for five minutes, then come back and cut out half of it again. Believe me, you will still have too much luggage, but you have to take a few things. Just think of a crowded airport after a ten-hour flight with no luggage trolleys available. It works every time. Nowadays, I am the queen of carry-on, but with children, there is no getting around hauling a mountain of stuff.

Pack everything you think your children will need to feel comfortable in the hotel you may have to stay in for weeks before your new accommodation is ready. We always travelled with pillow cases. Put some of their favourite DVDs in the suitcase as well. Pack new toys or distractions (for yourself as well as the children) in your hand luggage so you can dole them out along the way.

Have a lot of new smaller toys and books wrapped up like presents for the airplane (so your children will not discover them in the bag and ruin their distraction value). Take along two of everything in case something important gets lost, like a pacifier. (My daughter's pacifier fell out of her mouth and down an airplane toilet when it was just the two of us travelling together. Luckily I had a spare because someone had given me this advice—and I had taken it.)

Knapsacks are a good idea not only for your children's things, but for you too. If everything is on your back, this leaves your hands free to chase a child or carry something last minute.

Medical supplies

By this point, you may be thinking I am totally compulsive, but I have learned a lot of lessons the hard way. When it comes to medical supplies, especially if you are headed for a developing country, you can never be over-prepared.

I always pack two medical kits, one for the airplane and one for the suitcase. For on board: anti-nauseants and antihistamines for children to help them sleep (but remember you have to experiment and pre-test baby medicine), bandages, antacid tablets for airline food, eardrops just in case, eye drops for jet-lagged eyes, sleeping tablets (too optimistic, but you never know, and they do help you get over jet lag), baby aspirin (or anything else to bring down an in-flight fever), a thermometer, throat lozenges, lip balm, and extra-strength adult Tylenol. In the suitcase, I pack the heavier items: a rainbow assortment of cold medicines, antiseptic cleaner, mentholated chest rub for colds, vitamins, anti-diarrhea medicine, sunscreen, and topical ointments for every emergency. Also pack anti-malarial drugs if you are heading to a destination where disease-carrying mosquitoes are prevalent. A good mosquito repellant often works just as well.

Some Final Pre-Departure Advice

Common sense is your best defense against drowning in the tidal wave of emotions and physical exhaustion that may be plaguing you at this pre-departure stage. Listen to what your own inner voice is telling you. Always remember that you *do* know what is best for your family and for yourself, so take the time to follow your own intuition. Instincts you have always relied upon at home need not be abandoned, just modified to reflect a change of surroundings.

Recognize your jittery mood and quick temper as being merely part of a temporary condition that will go away. The house will get packed up, and you will actually say goodbye and board the airplane eventually. In fact, wait until you experience the sweet feeling of relief when you are on your way and there is nothing more to be done until you get where you are going. Savour that feeling.

It is always easier to say than do, but try not to be too hard on yourself. If your ability to be flexible momentarily disappears because you are exhausted, it will return when you have had a good night's sleep. Give yourself a few minutes to enjoy the thought of the exotic adventure that lies ahead. And remember this: were Superwoman moving overseas, even she would have to stop and shake off a bad mood before carrying on with what works best for her.

2 When You Arrive
How to Hit the Ground Running
Without Getting Your Face Smashed

"**M**om says there is no way she is ever doing this again," seven-year-old Lilly announced to her father after stepping off the Dragon Air flight from Hong Kong to Beijing.

"Hi, dear." That was all I could manage to mutter. My resentment and exhaustion combined to give me a kind of distorted look of despair. "We made it." Barely.

My daughter was confirming a theme I had mentioned too many times to my children during the marathon of flying we had just survived over the previous three days. ("Remember I said this," I ranted. "I'm never doing this alone again. I must have been crazy to agree to this!") My husband had headed out to Beijing two weeks ahead of his "dependents." I had chosen to remain behind in Canada, ensconced at a rented cottage, absorbing and savouring a few extra weeks of Canadian summer culture. It had been marvellous and therapeutic after a stressful year in Taipei. In Canada, we could be like the party people in the beer commercials, except without the beer: the last to leave the beach, the compulsive gas barbecue users, the credit card abusers.

Arriving at Beijing's then sleepy and less than upscale airport, especially after Hong Kong's old, crazily frenetic Kai Tak (the airport old-timers wax poetic over because you could literally reach out and touch the laundry hanging off an apartment building in Kowloon), I was not a pretty sight. I was a woman who had just flown halfway around the world, on non-stop flights of twelve hours or more, with two young children, too much luggage, and too little mental energy to absorb yet another change in housing. To break up the journey, I had stopped in both

Vancouver and Hong Kong, only to check in and out of hotels in what felt like a matter of minutes. Not unlike other travelling wives who do this every year, especially in the summer, I looked like a woman on the verge of a nervous breakdown. I was cranky and would have contemplated divorce if I did not love my husband so much.

My children travel extraordinarily well but moments will always occur. On this particular voyage, besides the expected stresses of a long door-to-door journey, there had been a few surprises too. Halfway over the Pacific, for instance, my daughter had bitten into an almond, forcing a gush of blood to come shooting out of her loose front tooth. Climbing over my sleeping son, I had stood on the arm rests in what could only have been perceived by fellow passengers as a hostile pose while attempting to yank the tooth from her mouth. The tooth would not budge. I looked like an airborne child molester. My worldly daughter, meanwhile, wondered aloud if the tooth fairy would leave a reward in Canadian or Hong Kong dollars.

It remains my firm belief that women should not leave home without two of everything their children could possibly need along the way and that definitely includes parents.

You Made It

At last, after months of taking care of the endless details of an international move (which in the real world would qualify you for a job as a chief executive officer of a major corporation), you are now about to tackle the challenge of settling into a new city, a new culture, new living quarters, a new life.

The arrival period will make demands on your physical and emotional stamina that will rival your pre-departure hysteria and can sometimes push your endurance to the wall. You may not be smiling upon arrival, but there truly will be more smiles in the future. Honestly.

No matter how many times you move overseas, no matter how prepared you are to face those initial feelings of temporary limbo, regardless of developed or developing setting, the first few weeks in your new environment will be disorienting until you find you and your family's new life rhythm and routine. The good news is that like any other phase in your life, the transition has a beginning, middle, and an end.

To be aware of what faces you, once you step off that airplane, will go a long way towards helping you to cope not only with the many changes in your life, but also to see them as part and parcel of the overseas adventure you will be bragging about to your friends back home in the annual Christmas letter. Today's trauma will be tomorrow's humorous dinner party anecdote.

Still, it cannot hurt to take note of a few of the emotional hurdles you are expected to clear before the laughing part begins. So here are some of the possibilities for tears and tantrums, and I am not just talking about your children's.

Airport Hassles

I have always felt that if a marriage has managed to survive long-distance flying, then foreign airports offer one final test of mettle. During our initial trip out to Taipei (with two parents in constant attendance of our children), I tested fate by becoming almost smug about how things had gone so well. We had flown without incident all the way through to Tokyo, where we had all managed to get a little sleep (with the help of a lot of baby anti-nauseant for our son) at a nearby airport hotel.

The next morning, somewhat refreshed and in high spirits, we had stuffed our faces with a hearty breakfast before catching the shuttle bus back to Narita Airport for our final flight to Taipei. The sun was shining, we were laughing with excitement, and we even waved as the shuttle bus pulled away after dropping us at our terminal. Then it hit me: the bus had made off with one of our suitcases and was already out of sight as it hustled itself back to the airport hotels for more passengers.

Naturally, I burst into hysterics (delayed reaction to sleep deprivation was my only plausible excuse). Defying the possibility of cardiac arrest, my husband took off at high speed after the bus, only to run in a circle around the departure area. There were phone calls, more hysterics, and announcements for flights were echoing around us while my children eyed me in complete shock, wondering whether to laugh or cry. We eventually got our bag, but I was not too impressive that morning.

Arriving in a foreign airport offers a particular challenge, because alongside often high temperatures can be crowded, suffocating, and completely overwhelming cultural conditions. These usually come in the form of a thousand screaming men all offering you a cheap taxi fare to the nearest city. And no matter the country, there may be long lineups for immigration, and luggage carousels giving no indication of which flight's luggage they carry. Add to that a typical worldwide lack of luggage trolleys and often ornery customs officials, and you can count on feeling like you have landed, exhausted, on another planet.

For a woman who probably stepped onto her first flight in a relatively cool and crisp state of mind and apparel, such airport scenes can eat at the last of her emotional reserves, especially if her partner has gone ahead and she is arriving solo, or she is weighted down by children. (This, at any rate, is my rationalization for my frazzled emotional state on arriving in Beijing.)

Whether I am alone or even with my spouse, I make sure somebody is waiting outside the customs and immigration hall to whisk us away. If you are with a company or represent your government, an official will likely be on hand to help you through the maze, especially if you make a request in advance. If nobody official is standing by, most airlines have representatives whose job it is to help arriving passengers with disabilities. Young children, in this instance, mean you qualify.

On our first posting, an opportunity to accompany my husband on a business trip to Burma (Myanmar) came up. I decided to overlook the fact that I was seven months pregnant and likely doing the most foolish thing I had ever done in my life. When we deplaned in Rangoon (now Yangon) from Bangkok, a journey some travel writers have described as one hour and thirty years, I was so overcome by the heat and time warp sensation brought about by the colonial-looking airport that I felt like fainting. Standing on the runway, enveloped by a humid fog, was our Burmese official, draped in the traditional sarong and waving a small Canadian flag at us. I thought I was delirious, but he relieved us of our passports (much to our initial dismay) and whisked us through customs in record time. Always try to make sure someone meets you at the airport.

Hotel Life

It is rare that your living accommodations are ready for you instantly upon your arrival, so be prepared to camp out in a hotel or empty service apartment for a few days, which may turn into a few weeks.

At the beginning of your assignment, a hotel room, lobby, and restaurant are just institutional reminders that you are not settled properly yet. Waking up in the middle of the night in a hotel room, and then suddenly remembering where you are, can be an unhappy experience too. I remember my own middle-of-the-night crying jags in fluorescent-lit bathrooms all too well.

To make the temporary accommodation easier to bear, pack as many familiar, homey items (the smaller the better) in your suitcase as you can. Framed pictures of your family, your child's favourite stuffed toy, or even a photo album will go a long way to easing your feelings of homesickness. You may also miss being able to make a cup of tea or have a drink that does not cost an arm and a leg from the hotel refrigerator. Wherever possible and if budget permits, reserve an apartment hotel room with kitchen facilities. They are often as reasonably priced as major hotel rooms. If apartment hotels are not available, seek out the nearest supermarket and load up cheaply. Room service loses its appeal when you feel like having a snack after a hot bath and are not keen to open your door half naked to a waiter.

One word of advice if you go the service apartment route: check out the amenities beforehand if possible. Upon arrival at our second assignment in Taipei, we found ourselves in a half-finished one. There was no restaurant except for an over-priced food kiosk in the unfinished lobby.

Laundry can be another issue if your company is not footing the bill for costs related to your hotel stay. Hotel laundry service is expensive, especially in cases where the cost of washing a two-year-old's T-shirt can be the same as cleaning a man's suit. Most hotel bathrooms come equipped with a small clothesline, which helps contain the sight of drying rinsed-out underwear to an out-of-the-way (and out-of-sight) location. Check the tele-phone book for the nearest laundromat if you are responsible for paying for it.

Despite the initial novelty, children find it hard to camp out in hotels. This has less to do with the rooms themselves than with the transference of the parent's tension from being con-fined to small quarters and eating meals (always *en famille*) only in restaurants. The following is sometimes easier to say than do depending where you are posted, but try to arrange activities special for children (errands definitely do not qualify) outside of the hotel to lessen the cabin fever that your family, and in par-ticular you and your spouse, may be feeling.

Being trapped in a hotel room with children to entertain while your husband goes to his new office can also be fraught. I confess: I am no good at all at hanging around all day with kids when I am feeling desperate to move into a new place and get organized.

We were put up in Beijing's Great Wall Sheraton while awaiting our move into one of the foreign compounds. (I will get to the deep stress brought on by the sight of your home in a minute.) Despite the hotel's five-star status, I found my blood pressure rising, pumped up by my resentment towards my husband (the guy with the job) and too many room service cups of coffee. By the end of the day, as I awaited his return, having no one with whom to share my frustration, my poor daughter had to listen to her mother's unrelenting advice: grow up to be a man if you know what is good for you.

One final word about hotel life: avoid the soaps. Hotel soap can be highly perfumed, like the bubble bath, and if you have sensitive skin, the soap will wreak havoc with your face. Three days into our hotel stay in Taipei, my face broke out in welts from the hotel soap. Imagine how much fun it was for me to be in a new city, with young children, barely over jet lag, and unable to face myself in the mirror without becoming completely undone.

Shaking Off Jet Lag

Jet lag miracle cures are as common as diet books. Like weight loss programs, though, they require incredible self-discipline, especially if you follow the most popular cures, which involve eating on alternate days or some such nonsense.

I say nonsense only because when you are moving abroad or arriving in a strange city, the last thing you want to do is add some strict regimen to an already overloaded emotional agenda. In my view, the extent of your jet lag will depend less on the number of time zones you move through and more on the number of children you are travelling with and the effectiveness of baby anti-nauseants. Jet lag is no myth, so you will feel tired and your stomach will be upside down until you get used to the change of water and food. The key to a quick recovery often lies in getting at least two nights' solid sleep of eight hours in order to turn your system around.

You do not have to be as strict as the jet lag diets advocate, but do keep your eating down to a minimum. Give your stomach time to get over all the airplane food. You will have plenty of time to sample the local fare. Tea and toast are good bland bets.

Timing Your Arrival

The timing of your arrival is important, especially if you are travelling with school-age children. If you are moving in the summer, inquire ahead of time to discover when the school term begins. Give your children about a week to get over their jet lag and enjoy the initial honeymoon of being in a new city, but arrive no earlier. Nothing to do at home is a lot different from nothing to do overseas when you are trying to get organized and feel guilty about parking young children in front of a television, a DVD player, and a stack of cartoon DVDs or movies. Likewise, do not arrive the night before school starts and expect your children to go off willingly alone the following morning on a strange school bus. Would you, as an adult, be brave enough to venture out immediately into the great unknown?

Many expatriate communities clear out in the summertime for extended home leave. This could mean that if you arrive too early, even with the best intentions of finding new friends from the foreign community for your children or for yourself, you will come up short. Such a situation will only fuel your family's feelings that they have left their friends behind and cannot meet any new ones. Since the object upon arrival is to connect with new people, it can be disheartening to discover that there is literally no one to meet. However, you can turn these circumstances into an opportunity to befriend local folk, especially in parks or playgrounds where other mothers may be out in the morning trying to entertain little ones. Local coffee shops are another place to start up a conversation. There will naturally be language barriers in some cases, but depending on the country, you may find someone who understands you enough to get both a conversation started and a feeling on your side that you are making even the slightest contact with your new culture.

You can always act like tourists while you wait for the residents to come back. You may be exhausted from your travelling, or you may think you have lots of time to see the sights. Neither excuse is good enough; getting out and seeing your new environment will actually help combat your fatigue, which may be from sleeping too much due to boredom. Also, old hands anywhere will tell you that often you just never get around to seeing what your city is famous for, so why not start right away? It certainly is a way of getting out of the hotel or an empty apartment awaiting its furniture. At the very least, it may reinforce some of the reasons you had for choosing your particular overseas location.

Walk, walk, and walk some more. I did so much of that when we first moved to Bangkok that one day, when my husband phoned home to check up on me, our lovely helper, Suporn, told him: "Madam walked out." That gave him a nice moment of panic! Soak up some local colour, even if it is only a quick run outside to buy a newspaper or some aspirin. Begin familiarizing yourself with the sounds and smells you will be living with for several years. Resist any urges to be a wimp and hide away in a hotel room. The sooner you venture out alone, the sooner you will regain your own feelings of independence and self-confidence.

Companies That Can Help

We moved to overseas postings four times and our arrival experiences were all different. The first time out, we were spoon-fed by an embassy support system that further introduced us to an extraordinarily sensitive spouse, who to this day is my guide to what an ideal foreign service wife should be like. In fact, she was so nice I could not believe she was real. On arrival at our first posting, albeit without children, we were wined, dined, introduced to both professional and personal contacts, and provided with a superb guide to the city's goods and social services, all within the first week.

The second time out to Taiwan was under slightly different circumstances, and such a comprehensive support system was not part of the package. We were the first ones into a unique situation, and certain prerequisites and support systems were voluntarily forfeited in return for the adventure of being trailblazers. We had no support, practical or emotional, and certainly nothing like the kind we had experienced on our first assignment overseas. I confess that I will take the spoon-feeding any day over the indifference. Our other moves fell somewhere in between in matters of support.

Even with offers of help, new arrivals often do not want to risk imposing on those around them. All I can say is this: go ahead and impose. The people you are feeling insecure around suffered the same feelings of isolation when they arrived and are more willing to help out than you may think.

While you cannot control or select the people who will be on the other end to help you, you can control your expectations of what will be done for you. If you go out expecting a band to greet you at the airport followed by a ten-course banquet in your hotel room, you will obviously be disappointed. If you expect very little assistance in getting settled, then what you do receive will be an unexpected bonus. Besides, the sooner you learn how to do things for yourself, the easier life overseas will become for you, because resourcefulness is a basic requirement to see you through those early days and the later ones too.

Fortunately, there are now literally thousands of professional relocation companies, coaches, and consultants, as well as community service organizations established in most foreign cities that cater to the orientation needs of just arrived expatriates. If you're on your own, without any organizational support, find one of them. In most cases, foreign embassies, international schools, even local churches will know about them. Or a local website offering country- or city-specific information will be a lifeline.

Many of these companies offer what are known as in-country orientation programs and they will cater their services to your needs. Often, if you are allowed a "look-see" visit before your move, it will have been coordinated by such a company. These professionals will teach you some of the basic survival skills you will need, such as knowing where the hospitals and grocery stores are, or introduce you to your host culture, through lectures or briefings. It is worth it to touch base with these professionals, because they can assist you not only at the beginning but throughout your stay as well by offering counselling, language training, and other adult education classes. They are usually the people who also will provide work permits, visas, and translation services.

Meeting the Boss and His Wife

At this end of the moving cycle, compared to before leaving home covered in the previous chapter, meeting the boss and his wife can be a shakier experience. Your mind may be numb from lack of sleep or distracted by details. You may also be quietly excusing yourself to go to the bathroom on the hour because of something you ate on the plane.

In short, this is not the greatest of times to meet someone who could have a say in your husband's career. Unfortunately, if you bow out of any early meeting (and you cannot do it indefinitely), that does not look too good either. Instead, keep this thought in mind: the boss's wife is also a woman who probably went crazy for a while when she first arrived. She may be more sympathetic than you think. All your worries about the kind of impression you are making could just be in your own head and not hers. She may have issues of her own, but you would not know it from just looking at her. As a therapist so aptly put it to me once, women so often decide how they feel on the inside by judging someone's outside.

You are at a vulnerable stage in your life, so do not expect miracles from yourself. If being you means being a distracted, sleepless, freaked-out lady, that is all right too. Just try to keep your insanity to a minimum.

Other Survival Tips for Early Days

About three days after arriving in Beijing, I was ready to see the foreign diplomatic compound we were scheduled to shortly move into. Our sojourn in the Chinese capital was long before the modern days of beautiful foreign housing complexes, with names like Beijing Riviera (and I am not making that up), built outside the city with schools nearby and Starbucks a stone's throw away. In the early days, post-Tiananmen, all foreigners were required to live in special compounds, which, surprisingly, provided an even playing field, as *everyone* lived in battered old housing. No one had anything special. Indeed, a visitor could enter another apartment and marvel aloud: "Oh, look what you've done with your dump. Lovely!"

On the day my husband took me to see what would be our home for the next two years, I only *thought* I was ready to face it. From behind the glass windows of the hotel, a dozen storeys up, life in China seemed pleasant enough. Stationed on what I started calling "Moon Station Beijing," with satellite television beaming us strange commercials from California, and frequent room service coffee trays, I had not seen much at ground level. Until we took a taxi to Jianguomenwai, a run-down group of a dozen apartment blocks in which foreign diplomats and journalists were kept a safe distance from the Chinese masses.

My brain froze, refusing to accept this new reality, especially at the outside of our building, which had steel bars surrounding our ground-floor apartment and giant dumpsters front and centre, overflowing. I simply was not ready for the sight of what, to me anyway, looked like a low-income housing unit. Spying the filthy, garbage-laden entranceway into our own apartment did not make matters better. Cruising by the "playground," littered with old equipment from McDonald's, which also gave the play-ground its name, I started to picture every kind of disaster that could befall my children.

My negative attitude towards the playground only got worse after one Jianguomenwai dweller laughingly told me about an incident in the playground: two African children got into a fight, and when their diplomat fathers came out to settle the matter, one killed the other. Who knew if the story was true or an urban legend, along with the story of a wife who jumped off the roof of the building behind us? I wanted to run away.

If you are in a developing country, as China certainly was back then (and still is once you leave the golden, gilded cities of skyscrapers), there may also be household helpers standing by to do your every bidding, including your cooking, shopping, cleaning, and babysitting. If there are no children to get orga-nized, or they are already off to school, you are sitting on your brand new couch, watching the help watch you. It is only seven o'clock in the morning and your spouse has already left for work. You wonder what to do next. Here are some ideas.

Do something nice for yourself

I am not into manicures or beauty treatments in general, but under certain circumstances they represent the ideal pampering tool. Go for it. Or go for anything that makes you happy: a new piece of clothing, an hour by yourself away from the family, a piece of chocolate cake in the hotel lobby or nearest bakery.

Another suggestion (and I am not being trite): never over-look the importance of escapist novels during the post-arrival period. You likely never had a chance to read before you left home, and the airplane may have had other distractions (like the need to constantly entertain children). Now that you have a little time on your hands that cannot be filled with anything too useful until your shipment arrives, sit back and read a book. Just do not spend all of your time in fictional never-never land. You cannot blot out your new environment forever. Likewise, do not get stuck in a virtual bubble of e-mail or Facebook. More on that in the next chapter, which focuses on culture shock, including the impact the digital age has had on it.

Avoid temptation

Spouses without children often find the late afternoon the hardest part of the day to deal with, especially early on when they have few friends to call up for a chat. The daytime hours at the beginning can be filled with long walks and errands, but dusk provides a different challenge, because there could be several hours when you are awaiting the return of your spouse from work. Some women confess they find themselves pouring a glass of wine to pass the time, and quickly find they have consumed several glasses before they know it. It is best to leave an activity, a walk around the block, or any form of exercise, for that matter, for those end-of-the-day hours.

Day trips

Depending on your spouse's work, the early days can often offer familiarization trips outside the city, to a factory, a branch office, or hospital. Wherever possible, arrange to go along on those trips so that you can also familiarize yourself with your host country and some of the problems it may be facing. It is refreshing to get an outside perspective and discover that the country itself may be far different from its capital city. You may also get to meet some of your husband's new colleagues, which will help when he starts talking about them. You will be able to put faces to names.

Start your photo collection

Many photographers who move abroad will tell you to take pictures within the first six months of your arrival in a new country. That is the time when things still look fresh to you. Often, after you have lived somewhere a while, you start to overlook the sights that startled you in the beginning. If you plan to make a visual record of your stay, begin as soon as possible. This is a good project for the early days. The same can be said for journal writing. While you may continue to jot down memories later on, write when your observations are the freshest.

You Have Not Invented Resentment

A journal is also a benign outlet for the feelings of frustration and resentment that you may be feeling towards your spouse. At least the paper cannot get into an argument with you. I have met a lot of accompanying spouses and have not yet found one who did not at one time or another feel overwhelming resentment towards their spouse for bringing them to some "godforsaken place!"

In the early days, it is also not unusual to go around screaming "It's your fault!" at your spouse, blaming him for everything from a stained blouse to a bad haircut and, of course, the fact that you feel overweight and out of shape. Resentment is usually at its most intense soon after you arrive. For one thing, after the travelling is over and all the adrenalin has stopped pumping, your emotions tend to come crashing down in the worst way. These are also the days when you are at your most vulnerable. You have left your friends and family behind, your environment is still strange and unfriendly, and you are in a waiting period until your new life takes shape.

If you are a naturally independent person, you may resent the feelings of dependence you have on your spouse, for money, for transportation, for entertainment, even for his help in making a doctor's appointment. If you are a career person who has put yours on hold or abandoned it altogether, there will be further resentment.

If someone can come up with a surefire method of avoiding these feelings, they could make a million dollars patenting it or win the Nobel Prize. Allow me to offer a piece of advice that I believe has kept my marriage to a travelling husband solid now for almost three decades: I am *not* dependent. We, as a couple, are *interdependent*. I came up with this years later (it is *always* years later) after one evening when I was feeling especially low about my life. Sensing my mood, Rodney told me that he simply could not do *his* job (at the time, post–foreign service, he was marketing Canadian educational institutions to foreign students, and that required a lot of travel) if I was not doing *my* job, which was looking after our home and our children. We operated then, as now, as a team. This mind shift certainly helped me delete the word "dependent" from my vocabulary and could help you.

Until the interdependent idea really sinks in, though, the only way around your feelings is to recognize the particular reasons that fuel resentment and then work out a strategy for avoiding them. From experience, I have identified three factors that often encourage resentment at the beginning of your posting and also offer some coping mechanisms.

1. Isolation

After culture shock (which I will deal with in chapter 3), feelings of isolation are highest on my list of conditions that used to feed my antagonism towards my husband. I blamed him for taking me away from everything that was familiar, comforting, easy to handle, and capable of making me act like a normal person instead of someone with wild mood swings. When I am isolated (by myself, feeling sorry for myself) I am no good to anyone.

Arguments were always pointless because, after all, we were there to stay so what was the use of saying everything is better back home? The only solution was to end the isolation by making the new environment familiar, comforting, and easy to handle, and by turning myself back into a normal person with only occasional mood swings. (I never said I was perfect.) As much as it may frighten me, I used to make the effort to learn about my new surroundings by getting into a taxi or going for long walks where I would make countless useful discoveries: there is the post office, there is the bookstore, there is a store selling my favourite makeup, and so on.

Returning from all those walks, I would invariably bring something back home that made our apartment or house friendlier, more inviting, like colourful fans for the walls, baskets for plants, pillows. You do not need a lot of money for these little outings, but make sure you bring your confidence, especially if you are posted to places like Seoul or Tokyo that have no street names.

To make my life easier to handle, I also would establish a routine, such as nap with my son: 12:00 to 1:00. Work at gaining control over some part of your day and let the rest fall into place. To make friends, each person has to come up with their own strategy that fits their personality, but as a general rule overseas, do learn to make the first move and to introduce yourself. Find a common point of interest and make a date to get together. Do not just say it, either: set a day on the spot. Isolation quickly ends when people come into your life.

2. Money

A fly on the wall of an overseas household could tell great tales about arguments over money and how all those overseas benefits should be spent. A more common sore point can be the resentment spouses may feel if they are given an allowance when they live away. Many women prefer to keep some personal channels of banking open to avoid what can be tight financial control overseas by their husbands. Since both my husband and I have always kept our budget controlled by allowances, I have never minded them, but have always used credit cards as an escape valve.

On our posting in Taiwan, I faced a cash-only society in those pre-ATM days. I had to think fast before I got too depressed. A solution was found that could work for others: have money assigned only for your use that is completely outside of funds you use for the necessities of life. Call it what you like—pin money, fun money, screw you money—just make sure *you* get to decide how it is spent. The important thing is to reach an agreement with your partner so the money issue does not become a major source of resentment between you.

3. Career

Except for couples who go overseas to work as husband and wife teams, such as foreign aid workers, military couples, World Health Organization medical officers, missionaries, and many teachers, most of the time, accompanying wives with careers back home gave them up to follow their husbands abroad. If you have put your career on hold to travel, you could now be resenting the hell out of your spouse for it.

For some reason, the reality of such decisions never really hits home until you are in your new house and have no office to go to or deadline to meet. It sounded great telling your friends before you left that you were going to look for something new or take a sabbatical, but once you are overseas, you find you are devastated the first time someone asks you what you do and you are tongue-tied for a response.

The bad news is that you will probably never get over giving up a career, so either get used to it or find something else to work at. The good news is nobody will likely ask you what you do. I am not being cynical about this, just truthful. In overseas settings, especially where working can be hassled and benefits for some families are high enough that a spouse is not forced to find a second income, women are rarely asked whether they are working, have worked, or even hope to work. That is not to say you will not meet local working women and be envious of their situations, but full-time working spouses overseas (many find part-time employment) are still the exception rather than the rule. This means your feelings of resentment will not be sparked too often by outsiders, but will most likely be your own demon to deal with.

Don't Be So Hard on Yourself

There can be no perfect score in clearing all the emotional hurdles that will lie in your path when you move abroad, so go easy on yourself. Just as I advised you to have as few expectations as you can of the welcome you will receive, by the same token, give yourself a break and temper your own expectations of yourself, your spouse, and your children.

Especially at the beginning, you and your family are dealing with a lot of anxiety and strain. Perfect behaviour, whether it is table manners or sensitivity, just cannot always be delivered. Likewise, do not get upset over your weight, your hair, or your clothes. Worrying about them can make your life miserable if they blow up on you. (I felt that face rash I got in Taipei merited some self-pity, but I managed to get past it with the help of a lot of will-power and strict avoidance of mirrors.)

Your environment may also not live up to your expectations if you set the bar too high. Your new home will not be like the home and country you left, so the sooner you start accepting the changes in the way you live, the better off you will be. Learn to substitute local products for the ones you preferred at home; find new areas of interest and new friends to replace the ones you left behind; stop yourself from making constant comparisons between old and new—schools, housing, everything, in fact—which could ruin your new life for you.

You have moved physically, and the sooner you move mentally too, the better you will feel. It is completely counterproductive, to say nothing of a waste of a good overseas posting, to spend all your time recreating your old environment. Remember this message I deliver to all of my audiences on all my speaking tours: It is a privilege to live abroad. But even living a privileged life does not mean you are not allowed to have challenges. How long you allow yourself to dwell on them is the real test of character.

You Will Get Settled Eventually

It will not happen overnight, but gradually street corners, shops, even traffic will become familiar to you and "back home" will become thoughts you take out and enjoy occasionally, like a family photo album. Your phone will start ringing again, your calendar will be filled, and you will find yourself out for an evening with good friends you suddenly realize you have known for less than two months.

You may not believe it, but it will happen. Your shipment will arrive, your home will assume a more cluttered air, your children will be out with friends, you may even get used to hot and spicy food, plain boiled food, or lots of fried food, depending on which part of the world you are in. The arrival period that seemed so endless, like all those flights it took you to get there, will be over so that finally you can get on with the adventure of life abroad.

3 Making the Cultural Transition
Having the Shit, Literally,
Scared Out of You

I once wrote the script for a briefing film for Canadian foreign aid workers going overseas. The program was titled *Culture Shocked!* Its purpose was straightforward enough: to help identify and ease the challenges of cultural transition.

Before writing the voice-over for the opening sequence, I forced myself to drift back to our first posting to Thailand to retrieve my memories of my initial experience with culture shock. Though it had been many years earlier, I was still able to conjure up a clear picture of the precise moment I stepped out of the airplane into a humid inferno that is the all-season temperature of Bangkok. Pausing momentarily at the top of a portable staircase (this was the early 1980s, the days of ancient airports and buses to ferry passengers to the terminal building) I gazed blindly into the cloudless sky, uneasy on my feet after the long haul, and slowly and very carefully negotiated the steps. When I reached the bottom, with barely a moment to attempt a deep breath, I was briskly shoved from behind into the shuttle bus, which seemed to have neither front nor back, just a packed core full of menacing-looking people.

I was sure I had screamed *Help!* but my husband had just smiled reassuringly at me without speaking. My head felt like it was about to lose the blood that sustained it. My throat dried up. There was sweat running down my back (*Could backs sweat like that?* I remember wondering), and I frantically gripped my husband's arm while we were transported barely a few hundred yards to the main terminal building.

When the doors opened again, passengers who had sat politely on the airplane for several hours were suddenly energized enough to rush down steamy colourless corridors to ensure they were the first to be processed through an immigration lineup that seemed to stretch back to the tarmac. I knew I was going to vomit all over my hand luggage because my head and stomach were doing somersaults. I barely made it to an airport cleaner's closet before heaving my shock into a pail.

However, first impressions, even vivid ones like mine, are not the entire story of culture shock. I knew if I was going to write a twenty-minute film on the subject that would be helpful, I needed to fill in the gaps in my knowledge and was directed to a specialist in culture shock to help me with my research. This professional, a well-worn traveller himself, was then known as an "animator" in the briefing business.

Afterwards, I remember thinking the title suited him well, for in the most animated of states, he responded to my opening question "What *is* culture shock anyway?" with a truly succinct reply that captured the crux of the issue.

"Culture shock," he said, "is when you have the shit scared out of you."

I hesitated for a minute, slightly nonplussed. Then I remembered my own arrival in Bangkok and my subsequent love affair with the toilet in the early days of our assignment.

"You mean . . . like diarrhea?" I asked.

"I mean exactly that," he responded, before suggesting we name the film along this theme in the interests of accuracy.

A Human Earthquake

He was right, if rather graphic. One of the first signs of cultural disorientation can be a revolt of your insides, from both ends. You will struggle to remember what you have eaten (was it the airplane food?), what you may have had to drink with ice in it. Or perhaps you will blame malarial tablets or anything else new that you have ingested along the way. Any or all of those things may be the culprit. But never overlook the strong physical shock waves your body is being hit with, a response to the overstimulation of your new surroundings that can affect your body as well as your mind. You are being bombarded with strange new images, often in subzero weather or sweltering heat, with a cacophony of noise swirling around your head. The smells alone of a strange city can do a number on your tummy.

I met an Egyptian woman once who confided that while her culture shock to Canada was pretty limited after growing up surrounded by foreigners in the cosmopolitan city of Alexandria, she will never forget the surprise she felt when the temperature plummeted to minus forty degrees in Winnipeg, the first Canadian city she and her husband lived in. The surprise was the discovery that she actually preferred cold weather to hot, although minus forty was a bit extreme.

In another instance of culture shock, a Taiwanese friend, married to a Canadian diplomat, said the shock of arriving in clean, orderly Canada was compounded by the fact that rules of the road especially were actually followed by law-abiding, polite Canadians. Speaking of roads, even driving on different sides of the road can be so disorienting as to lead to a headache and nausea.

Certain social customs of the "host" country can often lead to bewilderment too. For example, in England, where handling the produce at the greengrocer's is practically taboo, many African, Asian, and Latin American wives have had the wrath of irate greengrocers descend upon them. Unaware of the custom, and used to selecting their own purchases at market stalls in their own countries, they had innocently touched the delicate tomatoes and other vegetables during their first "solo" attempts at shopping for food. Such abrupt initiation rites definitely do not relieve the angst of rookie expatriate wives. With similar strange scenes and attitudes, to you at least, swirling around you, it is no wonder you feel overwhelmed and giddy when you first arrive. You have fallen into a kind of phantom zone. A reality still exists out there but you are seeing a different view of it.

What Is Culture Shock?

Culture shock, to provide a less graphic definition, is an individual's first reaction to an uncertain and different environment. "Culture" is the new way of life to which you are being exposed; "shock" is your physical and emotional response to that different way of life. In every country of the world, people share a particular view about living. When you move to a new country, that view is different, often radically, from the view you are used to. A neophyte traveller often makes the mistake of believing that another country's view of life is the wrong view. Nothing could be further from the truth. In matters of culture, there is no right or wrong, only different. Keep that uppermost in your mind. Try to avoid becoming the Ugly Expatriate.

Everybody Suffers Culture Shock

Not even a seasoned traveller can step off an airplane in a strange city and make an immediate adjustment. When you are a tourist, you are paying good money to experience exotic adventure and a change from the humdrum everyday life back home. When you arrive in a foreign country, though, knowing you will be staying for a few years, the culture shock can be much more frightening and certainly will have a wider scope. You cannot just brush it off with the knowledge that it will all be over in a few weeks. You will have to live with the different smells, climate, language, traffic conditions, poor people, too rich people (that can shock you too, believe me), or any other signs of cultural differences that strike you upon arrival.

You Can Chart the Stages

Culture shock has a life cycle of its own, usually lasting about six months to a year. There are also very distinct stages, so be prepared by knowing how to identify them.

Tourist/honeymoon stage

This is the easiest of all the stages to recognize. You have just arrived. You may have been overwhelmed at the airport for a few minutes, but that was jet lag. Now everything looks charming. The hotel you are staying at provides a protective cocoon. The staff speak English and want to assist you. Everything is worthy of a photo, and talking to people on the street is fun, even if they are scaring your fair-haired children to death by pinching their cheeks, stroking their hair, or swarming them to take a photo. You jump into the new culture, eating everything in sight. Often you need the security of another person showing you around, but generally you are open to it all. The day-to-day hardships have not set in yet.

This stage usually lasts until you have been in your new house or apartment a few weeks. If you have a two-year-old in tow, as we did our second time out to Taipei, you usually skip this stage and go straight to the crisis stage, which is next.

Crisis stage

The novelty wears off. Nobody has a phone number that works. All those people showing you around at the beginning have resumed their own lives and expect that you will now get on with yours. Your frustration levels rise, as you try to put your house in order or sign up your kids for activities. You have spent an entire day trying to find something that will never be found. Things do not work and you feel you cannot explain to anyone what you need done. You feel like a child yourself, learning to speak again. If you find yourself lashing out in anger every few minutes, especially at your husband, you know you have hit the crisis stage.

Flight stage

So what do you want to do with all this hostility? Book a ticket online and head for the airport. Running away seems like a viable option, if not physically then mentally, into a novel that you read all day or socially, online, in the absence of new friends. You may try to forget entirely that you are overseas by immersing yourself in all those DVDs you brought along. The last thing you want to do is go out and do things or meet new people, even if that is ultimately the key to getting over your culture shock.

Period of readjustment

Relax! This is the end of the culture shock cycle. It is a condition that goes away like a bad cold. You do somehow emerge at the other end of the tunnel, even if the ride has been bumpy or made you ill along the way. You manage to chill out and life resumes a pattern similar to what you had at home, albeit with a different backdrop. You wake up, you plan your day, you live your life as best you can, and you remind yourself that one day in the future you will be able to tell great stories at a dinner party about the horrible culture shock you went through. Or write a book about it.

Culture shock in the digital age

New technologies can delay the process of working through these stages in order to come out the other side. I write about this at length in *Raising Global Nomads* but also want to offer a few brief highlights of my twenty-first-century research here.

In the early stages of your transition, the Internet and cell phone will become your most important life props. A local chat room can connect you to a woman's club, help you find household help, or just give you the local news. When used locally, these digital connections can be immensely helpful.

Be warned, though, that they can help create a false sense of connection. This can be especially true for children who are text messaging or chatting online with friends back home. Eventually, their friends (and yours too probably) will stop communicating daily or even weekly as you leave the sphere of their daily lives. As comforting as these connections may be, especially at the beginning, they are not happening in real time in a family's new real world. In the case of teenage children in particular, too much time spent in the wireless world could also lead to a lot of hurt feelings when messages start going unanswered. Distracting yourself by sitting at a computer "talking" with a friend thousands of miles away may fill the day, but it can create a dreamlike state that will not help you settle into your new locale.

In her work as a transition coach for expatriate families, interculturalist Barbara Schaetti also believes the Internet can become a hindrance rather than a facilitator when people rely on absent friends and family to the exclusion of peers in the new locale. It is the crisis stage of culture shock that has the biggest potential to be affected, Schaetti says.

"During the honeymoon phase, you're out in your new location checking things out, seeing all the commonalities. Your reports home are likely to be relatively happy ones, and you're not as likely to be glued to the computer waiting for a response as if you're feeling miserable and miserably misunderstood. But when people are in the crisis or flight stages, they're less likely to leap away from their computer, given the illusory appeal it offers of home community connection. Cultural learning won't happen, and they could get stuck in the crisis stage of culture shock. And without cultural learning," asks Schaetti, "why bother to have packed up your house and family in the first place? If there's no gain, it sure isn't worth the pain!"

Children who have been raised on text or instant messaging and cell phones may have a hard time breaking the digital umbilical cord with home or their previous posting. As parents, you naturally want your children to breeze happily through the early days of relocation. If communicating with friends back home pacifies them, you will find that hard to take away. But a friend over the computer or a cell phone is not a friend in the here and now.

Finally, remember something I stress in all of my lectures nowadays on this subject: cross-cultural experiences, growth, and the making of new friends simply will not happen in a cyber bubble.

Why Did I Come?

Depression, acute unhappiness, resentment, fear, loss of identity and privacy, longing for your own wonderful support system back home, and let us not forget crying, crying, crying: these are also the hallmark emotions of the onset of a wife's culture shock. In other words, you are scared out of your wits about making a success of your new life, but are desperately trying not to show it. Panic is written all over your face. Or you think it is, which is just as bad. You sit in a chair, staring off into space, chanting a dazed mantra: "Why the hell did I come here? Why the hell did I come here?"

Your husband, the reason you are in this situation, comes home from work and you jump all over him for reasons you know sound foolish even as you are saying them. For example, "The maid put the cutlery in the wrong drawer," or, my favourite, "I took the kids to McDonald's and it was awful! There were no napkins, your son spilled his milk, and nobody helped me with the stroller."

None of these are life-threatening situations, but they are exactly the kind of scenarios that throw you off balance. The larger issues in life you can handle; it's the minor details that irritate you out of your mind and make you think you want to go home. You have not even come close to understanding the host culture yet, but you know you hate it and want to leave. Hello, culture shock.

The Absent Husband

Life could be worse. Think of the women who have to handle the trauma by themselves, and there are many. Some wives watch their husbands go out the door for a weeklong trip only moments after they have arrived in the new country, leaving their wives to open bank accounts, stock the cupboards, and settle the children into school. Naturally, such trips cannot be postponed (a likely story), so many women are not only suddenly thrust into a new place, but also are left to deal with it entirely on their own. If that happens to you, make a friend as quickly as possible, perhaps a seasoned expatriate wife with a sympathetic face or a local neighbour to help you with the language barrier.

An Appearance of Sudden Wealth/Poverty

Depending on where you are living, that is, developed or developing country, another influence on your culture shock could be the sudden change in your standard of living from what you were accustomed to at home. Cars and drivers, household help, gardeners, luxurious houses or apartments are suddenly your new way of life; alternatively, laundromats, bicycle repair shops, and Do-It-Yourself stores could become new regular hangouts. You feel disoriented because you truly are living in a new world, both inside and outside your home.

When we were living in Bangkok, *The Jewel in the Crown* miniseries was opening people's eyes to the lifestyles of the colonial families of the British Raj. I had borrowed copies of the series from the local video shop and was watching an episode one day with another friend also assigned to Bangkok. During a scene in which Indian bearers were circulating at a party with cocktails for the expats, we were both remarking on the good life of the Raj. No sooner had we finished criticizing the laziness of those old India hands when my Thai maid knocked discreetly at the door. "Madam, I have your lunch," she said, entering with a tray laden with neatly laid out sandwiches and a pot of coffee. Whoops.

And What About the Children?

A week after we arrived in Taipei on our second posting, then six-year-old Lilly, always extremely well adjusted and mature for her age, suddenly burst into tears for no apparent reason. Her younger brother had not thrown anything at her; she was not coming down with something; she appeared normal if maybe just a little pale in the face. She had seemed to be enjoying the move so far, and I wondered what might have brought on the tears.

"I miss my friends!" she finally articulated to me after much coaxing.

"I miss my friends too!" I answered her, before going back to my motherly role and comforting this sad little girl.

Later, I thought about that particular day's events, searching for a clue as to what might have triggered her distress. Rodney and I had been given a brief orientation by a professional support organization. The children had been left for several hours with a babysitter so we could gather the information we needed without distraction. It was the first time Lilly had been separated from us, even briefly, in the entire three-week period we had been on the road travelling and resettling.

Kids Suffer from Culture Shock Too

My daughter experienced kiddie culture shock. Once I had made my diagnosis, I could see that both my daughter and my toddler son were experiencing similar symptoms of the adult version, if slightly modified for youthful concerns. My daughter had passed out of the honeymoon stage momentarily and reached her first "crisis," precipitated by a separation, not unlike the first time I had ventured out alone into the strange streets of a new city. She was feeling unsure of herself and insecure without a parent there to stabilize her. Hence, her tears and fears.

Toddler Jay experienced culture shock in a much more vocal way, as any normal two-year-old would do. A temper tantrum that continued for two months seemed to be his reaction to his new environment. I could hardly blame the little guy. In Canada we had been living in a rural environment where he saw maybe a dozen people a week, and suddenly he was in Taipei, where even in an elevator, there would be a dozen people sharing it with us, all poking and prodding him to death because of his white-blond hair.

Many children regress in reaction to the new culture. A toilet-trained toddler may suddenly wet his pants; a ten-year-old boy may suddenly need a stuffed animal to sleep with again; a fifteen-year-old girl suddenly wants to read in her room and not go out her bedroom door. In *Raising Global Nomads* I offer hundreds of pages of advice about raising expatriate children so will not dwell here on the subject of children and culture shock except to say that the three biggest losses contributing to a child's culture shock during transition are school, friends, and pets. Keep that in mind.

And I will offer only one piece of advice I wish someone had given me from the get-go: and that is, to hone my "happy voice" skill. It should be self-explanatory, but when informing your children of *anything* regarding the move, do so in a voice filled with lightness, happiness, and bonhomie (instead of darkness, anger, and resentment). This will go a lot further to ensuring a successful transition for a child.

Seasonal Culture Shock
Just when you think your children have adjusted to their new home, along comes a holiday that might plunge them back into a depression. During our first Christmas in Taipei, I could not understand why my otherwise happy daughter seemed so down and listless. Granted, her best chum in our apartment block had taken off for Hawaii for two weeks, but I kept feeling something else was on my daughter's mind. Finally I dragged it out of her. Christmas, she said, just did not feel right without snow. And why couldn't we have a real tree instead of that fake job from Toys-R-Us lighting up our living room? It just was not the same. She wanted to be in Canada—home to her—for Christmas.

For some children, not unlike their parents, making the cultural transition can be a year-round proposition, at least for the first year overseas. Watch for mood changes at holidays, birthdays, or other annual milestones, which may make your children long for the way in which such occasions were marked at home.

More Ways to Help Your Children

Patience is indeed a virtue, and never will it be the virtue it becomes overseas. Good luck! Do the best you can, especially if you have a toddler with you. Thoughtful gestures work well too. Here are a few other tried-and-true methods of dealing with kiddie culture shock.

Recognize the signs

A temper tantrum or soiled panties are the easy clues. Mood swings, unexplained tears, lack of appetite, and sleeplessness are also obvious signs. Less noticeable are the social signs that may happen while your children are at school. Discipline problems, inattention to homework, or the inability to make new friends because the old ones were nicer are all definite symptoms of a child's culture shock.

Some children, like adults, become more accident prone (and visit the school nurse's office a lot), or seem to be sick with flu or colds more often. Normally gregarious children who suddenly become sullen are also having problems of adaptation. I met a culture shocked child once who asked to see his parents' passports before they went out for the evening. He was afraid they were going to leave the country—and him—behind.

Routines can save the day

It may be difficult while settling in, but the sooner you establish a new routine for your culture shocked children, the better off they will be. The security of a schedule, bedtime especially, will help put a child back on track. School-age children are in the best position to get over this transitional period, because a day at school provides a timetable and fixed activities.

A toddler is more problematic (and I certainly know this from experience), but even my young son finally levelled out a few weeks after settling into a morning nursery school program. Weekends should also be structured as much as possible.

Familiar foods and other signs of home

Once your shipment from home arrives, with toys and other familiar knickknacks, life gets better for your children. While you cannot recreate home, and would not want to or the point of moving abroad would be lost entirely, it helps to reassure your children that life may have changed, but not completely. Food especially helps. It is possible in most countries to find food that approximates what my daughter used to call "normal" food, that is, anything they were used to eating at home, whether it is their favourite cereal, macaroni and cheese, or plain white rice. Sure, you would like them to eat other kinds of food, but do not offer it every day. If you can, try to alternate ethnic food with their food of choice.

Communicating is more important than ever

It is often easy to let your children's concerns get lost in the shuffle of organizing your new life, but now more than ever it becomes critical to really listen to and respect what your children are telling you. Their shock is as real to them as yours is to you. Indulge their whims a bit more than you may have at home, at least in the beginning.

I am not advocating we turn our expatriate children into spoiled brats (which is an easy pitfall), but their smaller fancies should be catered to, like the way they want to decorate their bedrooms, or their request for friends to visit even if it is not terribly convenient for you. New friendships will help your child adjust faster than anything else, so try to accommodate after-school play dates.

In the first weeks, it may be necessary to knock on doors around you to help your child connect with new friends. Be prepared to do that or to cold-call mothers on a class list to see if they are interested in getting the children together.

Teach them a few words of the new language

Your children may not need as much fluency in the local tongue as you will, but it does not hurt to try to teach them a few words so they can communicate a bit when they are settling in. Being a linguist of questionable ability myself, I have always found my daughter teaching me more language skills than I could ever teach her. But knowing the basics like "please" and "thank you" right away could help them feel less alienated from their new culture as well as be polite. If your children attend a local school, as do some children of missionaries and visiting scholars, it will not be long before they will be teaching you whole sentences *and* correcting your accent as well.

Parent-child relationships

Whatever your relationship was before you left home, be prepared to restructure it when you move abroad. To say you are now needed, when the idea would not cross your child's head at home, is an understatement. Parents are the constant, the symbol of stability and continuity, in an otherwise changing world. As a mother, you are thrust once again into an extreme nurturing situation, regardless of age. Your children need you *more* after relocation, not less.

When your teenager tells you that you have ruined her life by taking her away from her friends, you have to be patient and explain that while that may be true, such ruination is only short-term, like the duration of culture shock. When your toddler son embarks on an endless temper tantrum (and you secretly envy him for the fact that he can run around the room in circles crying, because you want to do the same), you have to recognize that what worked at home for discipline and general mothering may need to be modified overseas. Patience and a sense of humour are definitely the order of the day, even though on some days it will seem a very tall order to fill.

Parents' dynamics affect the children
If the parents are barely on speaking terms after two weeks in a hotel, having had no quality time together and attending to the endless paperwork and legwork involved in establishing a new household, imagine how that tension filters down to an uncertain and insecure child who has just been dragged to what seems like the ends of the earth. The most difficult task of all in helping your children cope with culture shock can be trying to act happy around them when the anxiety is mounting with each passing moment.

Likewise, taking out your adult frustration by shouting at your children just because they did something like jump on a hotel bed because they have absolutely no place to run is hardly going to make a child feel like he is ever going to adapt to his new environment. Make sure mommy and daddy are not as different in their behaviour as the street outside. A child once told me: "I think a different Mommy and Daddy came out of the moving boxes than went into them back home."

A Checklist to Deal with Your Own Shock
If you are going to get through it, and I cannot stress enough that culture shock is not a terminal condition, it helps to keep this survival checklist nearby for constant reference. It may not stop the tears, but it could help you get on with your new life overseas once the tears stop.

Participation is the key
The only way to become part of your new environment is to jump right into it and become an active participant. This does not have to happen the very next day after you arrive, but small

steps can be taken at first, like reading the local papers and websites to get a handle on the country's issues, or expatriate magazines or newsletters to see what the foreign community is all about. Later, after the dust has settled and your children are in school, you can seek out activities for yourself, whether that is a language course (a great way to meet other newcomers) or other life courses offered around town.

Joining a club like the YWCA if there is one, attending support groups, or helping out with your children's activities are other ways of joining in the local action. Talk with people you meet to find out how they keep busy. Volunteer work (in some countries) can be easy to find and will serve the dual purpose of helping yourself and others.

Seek support

Local community services centres have sprung up in many foreign communities around the world, offering courses on the host culture in addition to solid orientation advice and counselling services. Also, there are now expatriate transition coaches advertising all over the Web offering consulting via the Internet.

Do not be afraid to ask these professionals for free advice or even pay for the services of someone to assist you in your transition period. Ad hoc support groups, for young mothers or people with common problems, also abound and should be checked out. Consider these groups even if you have never belonged to one in your life. An international mothers' group in Bangkok, which helped organize playgroups or just provide the latest information on the availability of Pampers, practically saved my life, in addition to introducing me to some of the finest women I know. In cities where there are no professional organizations, start your own support group.

Establish new support systems

Feelings of isolation can be intense when you are far away from friends and family, so it is critical that you find new substitutes early on. This can be as simple as establishing one solid friendship with another woman you feel you can phone every day just to shoot the breeze or compare reactions to the new culture. Having someone you feel you can call in an emergency and especially if your husband travels a lot can ease a lot of your culture shock–related stress. Assemble your own new set of support "staff."

Appreciate cultural differences

You have moved to a new culture so do not shut it out. Neither should you make judgments based on five minutes of research. Remember that many of the cultures you may be dismissing out of hand have been around a lot longer than yours and deserve more than a cursory examination before you decide they are no good. Everyone has a different way of doing things, even back home within your own neighbourhood, so consider cultural differences as something positive rather than negative, worth learning and caring about to strengthen your own character and values. If you can, travel as much as possible to see your host country.

Many adjustments may have been necessary at home

On our first posting, we had our first child and our lives were thrown into the chaos only a baby brings to the home. While Bangkok likely exaggerated certain new restrictions in our lives, we would have had the same ones at home (but certainly not the inexpensive household caregiving help). Do not blame a bad marriage or a sour child-parent relationship on your new environment. Sometimes the new city may not help matters, but many problems and adjustments could just as likely have cropped up at home.

It's Not Just the Foreign Culture That Will Shock You

I was a guest at a dinner party near the beginning of our second posting abroad when I sensed something was missing from the conversation around the table. While the women were politely drawing out their male dinner companions on the subject of their careers, their past lives, and their general philosophy towards life and the host culture, the courtesy was not being reciprocated. So I tried to interject with a few references to my own career, past life, and general philosophy.

"I'm actually a journalist by training," I began tentatively, hoping that someone would care.

"So how's business for you?" one of the men inquired of the other, before I realized the cue had not only been ignored, it had been left to twist in the wind.

I decided to return to my fork and knife and angle for another entry point.

"You know," I tried again over dessert, "I've done a lot of work in corporate communications. I imagine there's a lot of proactive marketing of Taiwan going on around here."

There, I thought, some power talk

"That's nice," one man commented. "My wife weaves."

The Great Leap Backward

You think I am kidding. Sad to say, I am not. In many foreign communities overseas, a woman's feeling of disorientation, a key factor in culture shock, is often just as much a result of a time warp back to the days of the "little woman" as it is from tasting hot food or living with a billion people. It can be a double dose of culture shock: a reaction to the unfamiliarity of the foreign culture and alienation from your own as well.

I do not want to take anything away from the men assigned overseas who have no choice but to work long hours, because sometimes they just cannot help but leave their wives with the bulk of the responsibilities concerning the family. There is often little choice for them, especially now in a 24/7 work world where a BlackBerry is worn like an accessory around their waist. Likewise, I have seen firsthand the life of a busy diplomat who must wine and dine for his country at endless banquets or receptions, or travel with visiting widget salesmen or government ministers.

The question is: How do those men act once they come home? Do they instantly try to balance the equation? Or do they tell their wives they are too tired to go out and the wife is being selfish for asking, even if she has not been outside of her home for a week?

Here lies the separation between a loving husband and father and an SOB who has decided everything will be his way or no way during your overseas assignment. By the way, this latter personality type usually characterizes the ill-bred chaps who do not bother to ask a woman seated next to them at a dinner table if she ever had a professional life, or even an original thought, before moving abroad with her husband.

Where Is Gloria Steinem When You Need Her?

To cope with these dominant male attitudes abroad, you are certainly not expected to transform yourself into a mid-twentieth-century television mother overnight. To this day, I am still looking for a guidebook that prepares or even just acknowledges this social regression endemic to men in expatriate culture. If I hear the quip one more time by an expatriate male that in his next life he wants to come back as an expat wife, I could very well shoot the jokester. However, I think it is important to raise the issue in order that coping mechanisms, and not artificial ones, can be found.

Where do these male attitudes spring from? Voluntary withdrawal by the accompanying spouse from the workforce (often because spousal employment can be downright impossible, or inconvenient and hassled) as well as generous overseas allowances all can contribute to a lavish lifestyle and one-income marriages. They can also encourage a return to perceived prerogatives some men assume are automatically assigned to the Major Breadwinner, such as golfing all weekend or staying out late at night entertaining clients.

I have seen evidence and heard firsthand testimony that supports the idea that this Retro Macho Man may have been the most liberated of chaps at home. But once he hits the overseas life, the rules of equity vanish.

So Which Shock Should You Deal With First?

Adjusting to the foreign culture is definitely your first priority, since it may take a few weeks before the aftershocks from the new social condition sink in. Also, the shock of your own culture overseas, like the male chauvinism I just described, can be dealt with a lot more effectively after you are used to the host culture and your self-confidence has returned to previous levels. There is no point arguing a position until your feet are firmly planted on your new ground. Understand the basic strategies of fighting culture shock before tackling this corollary issue, that is, the battle of the sexes, which may develop in your own home.

And finally, never step out of your door without your sense of humour. If you cannot laugh at it all and especially at yourself for throwing temper tantrums over the most ridiculous things, there is no point in leaving the home.

4 Now What?
How a Spouse Can Avoid 'Nothing to Do' Syndrome

I can still vividly recall hanging around a New York apartment hotel room in sloppy jeans and a tumbled T-shirt while my husband strutted out the door in a new pinstripe three-piece suit, optimistically beginning his diplomatic career at the United Nations. After the door had slammed on Mr. Future Ambassador, I remember trying hard to rechannel my resentment energy into something constructive. But I could only unpack our suitcases for so long, since we had travelled light for a mere three-month assignment at the General Assembly. And I did not care to rearrange the hotel's furniture or decorate its bland institutional decor.

I did tackle something useful, stocking up the fridge, but ended up experiencing New York–style culture shock when I innocently wandered into a nearby grocery store and was robbed, not by a mugger, but by the owner's inflated idea of what can legally be charged for a lamb chop in midtown Manhattan.

Situated where I was, which was equidistant between Bloomingdales and Saks Fifth Avenue, it should have been a dream come true, for I was a newly married woman at the time, without children. And as a longstanding student of the Arts and Leisure section of the Sunday *New York Times*, I had waited years for just such an opportunity as I was being handed. But instead of excitedly racing out into the street, I chose to stare out my window at the back of the Waldorf Astoria Hotel and ponder the meaning of diplomatic life. I especially wondered what exactly was going to be in it for me.

What do I do with my life now, I asked myself, *now that I have given up (gladly, I had thought) my career as a television journalist?* The alternatives, in those early days as an accompanying spouse, seemed limited to over-eating, crying, throwing things at the television set when "news actors" instead of journalists presented the news, and desperately feeling like my world had collapsed. I had forgotten altogether that my friends thought I was the luckiest woman alive.

'Nothing to Do' Syndrome

Unknown to me at the time, since I was still a neophyte in my new role and lifestyle, I was falling victim to a fate that I would have shared with the colonial ladies of the British Raj. Not only did their experiences give rise to an official designation for dependents as the "useless mouths" (I tried to use that once on my passport application), but they also put a name to a condition thousands of travelling wives to follow would suffer from: "nothing to do" syndrome.

You certainly do not have to travel to suffer from it. But in some international settings, where there still may be a ton of household helpers attending to your basic needs, your husband and children are gone for the day, your house is decorated institutionally, and it is stifling hot or freezing cold outside your door, you may in fact sit down in a chair with a day stretching before you that has too many hours to fill.

Compounding matters further can be the early hour at which your foreign city awakens and begins its day. In many hot countries, life shuts down for rests or siestas after lunch, and in temperate countries, winter afternoons are as black as night. Some days will feel endless and empty.

It is true that while you are settling in, there are countless numbers of errands to occupy many of those hours. And if you have moved to a Western country and are facing daily life without household help for the first time, you may feel like you will never have any personal free time again. But when the last picture has been hung on the wall of your new home, the last piece of furniture purchased, the last drawer organized to perfection, the last child settled in school for the entire day or for just a few hours, and a routine finally established that frees you for at least a few hours a day, it is hard to avoid facing up to the next stage in your overseas adventure: *Now what* do I do with myself?

Everybody Asks Themselves This Question

First off, if you are pondering the "Now what?" question, be aware that you are not alone. Some may wonder about it for a minute, others for the length of the entire posting, but most wives who move abroad with their husbands will at some point ask themselves what they should do next. All the pre-planning in the world, all the enthusiasm for the local culture and people, will not cancel out the existential angst of the early days. Unlike the working half of the couple who goes to an office, or even youngsters who have the structure of the classroom, the spouse's life is completely uncharted and open to suggestion—and possibility. I am not talking here about the responsibilities associated with children, because they do not change no matter where you live in the world. They go with any territory.

Rather, I am referring to free time, the personal time to pursue whatever interests you, and only you. For some women, this could mean finding the nearest bridge game, golf course, or tennis court. For others, it could be volunteering at a local charity or cultural society. Still others will want to check out the local job market. Before you head off with your golf clubs or résumé, you may still likely experience a moment when you draw a blank, a dead time zone where you may find yourself sitting in a chair, staring out a window, and contemplating your new universe. You want to get moving onto something new but cannot seem to find the mental energy.

Worse still, you may be immobilized by the cultural stereotypes that await you outside your door. A Hong Kong Chinese woman I know who moved to the United States said she preferred to do nothing all day rather than face new people who reduced her to the cultural stereotype of a passive Chinese woman, content to be a mere toy for her Western husband. When this same woman moved to Taiwan, it bothered her even more to have people assume she married not for love, but for a U.S. passport.

If you feel like hiding out for the duration of your post, do not despair: you are not the first woman to be immobilized by apathy or stereotyping.

Before you can get to the point where you can overcome your own inertia, be aware that there may be many contributing factors you have not considered. Some of them are unique to overseas life, like the struggle to find good help to keep the dust from the Gobi Desert off your furniture, or the problem of incompatible electric currents, or just plain exhaustion from the move itself.

If you ignore these factors, and are just too hard on yourself, you risk not only prolonging your lethargy but giving yourself a massive dose of depression on top of it all. So, before you can get on with your new life abroad, you may first have to recognize and deal with a few feelings that are downright impossible to avoid.

Age and Stage of Boredom

A lot of the structured activities in your overseas life will depend on the age and stage of your life. If you have young children with you, it can be easier to plug into the community faster (by virtue of necessity). You will also find that the last thing you are suffering from is "nothing to do" syndrome. For the young mother, there will likely not be enough hours in the day to do everything you want to do (like relax, put your feet up for five minutes, or remember you are actually living abroad).

Without the responsibility of children, feelings of intense boredom are more likely to overwhelm women in the beginning. These spouses may find their husbands are out for long working days that stretch into evening entertainment, while they sit waiting at home—and then, of course, when he does come home he is glued to his computer or BlackBerry. It is critical to one's mental health to get focused on something that will keep the mind active. But first you must get past a question swirling around in your brain . . .

Who Am I?

One of the biggest existential headaches for spouses moving abroad is the temporary loss of the critical qualities that a woman needs to keep her ego from collapsing in total despair, namely self-confidence, self-esteem, and a sense of her own identity. In my experience, the first social invitation provides the litmus test for how those qualities are faring overseas. If you fail the test, you are in good company.

It does not matter if it is your first dinner party, cocktail party, or coffee morning, a good majority of women will decide at the last minute that they do not want to go! I use an exclamation point only because it will match most women's emotional condition at the point of their decision. The reasons for the refusal will vary: nothing to wear, hair needs to be cut but a trustworthy hairdresser has not been found, a perm has gone awry in tropical heat, exhaustion and lack of energy, inability to reciprocate while still unsettled, or a face that is a mass of welts from allergic reactions to hotel soap. The list of excuses will go on and on but they will share a common theme. You feel rotten about yourself. You feel invisible and inferior. You hate yourself and nobody could possibly like you. You are not budging, ever, from your hotel room, apartment, or house.

If your husband is standing by watching your self-flagellation (I should ask my own husband to add a footnote here), he will either be shaking his head or trying not to laugh. It is not funny to you, though, especially if you can remember a time long ago when you were a confident person who felt good about herself. When we moved overseas our first time to Bangkok, it would be an understatement to say that my self-confidence was at an all-time low. I wanted to stand at parties and hand out my résumé as a way of showing people that I was certainly a more interesting person than I appeared to be, which was a sweating, self-conscious, newly arrived wimpy-looking character, clutching a drenched purse (from holding it under my arm), frozen three inches from the hors d'oeuvres table. Soon after we arrived in Beijing (and I was supposedly getting good at moving around), I gave this post-arrival inferiority complex a name: "speck syndrome." Hi, I wanted to say and practically did, I'm nobody from nowhere: Ms. Speck of Dust.

It is the rare individual who can casually walk into a room to face strangers (even friendly ones) after just relocating her life thousands of miles. Absolutely nobody is that secure. It takes time to build up that security again.

When it dawns on you, however, that almost every woman who moves abroad must start from scratch to rebuild her shattered ego and actually manages to do so, your own self-confidence begins to return. You realize that like everyone else, you too will get past being the nervous newcomer. People will know who you are, remember meeting you or hearing about you from somebody else. Someone may actually remember that you have a skill of some sort and ask you to do something—bake a cake, give a course—perhaps even offer you a job. Events do eventually transpire to allow the return of your self-confidence.

In an overseas setting, though, you must make more of an effort. There is no built-in security blanket of friends or family, or even professional community like you may have had at home. You have to be more aggressive and open with people: ask questions, follow up with phone calls to arrange another meeting. Your ego is going through adjustments and will even out given the proper circumstances. Often just one new friend with common interests or an assignment of any kind will set you on track again.

My overseas Chinese friend, for instance, quickly realized that she would have to compromise a bit and attempt to be more outgoing in the United States than she would normally be at home. She also befriended a Filipina woman while living in Taiwan. Together they faced many of the same cultural attitude problems and could empathize with each other. Your self-esteem will be challenged throughout your posting, just as it can be at home, but a foreign setting can inflame inferiority complexes, and it will not be only successful women in the host culture who throw your self-image into the gutter. Often it is other expatriate women, who exude confidence and ability, who will get you down, especially when you are starting out in your new post and feeling unsure of yourself. You may meet some dynamo who has started her own export business of some rare local treasure, and you have not even been able to find raisins anywhere. On my first posting, when I still believed I wanted to be a foreign correspondent (motherhood helped me abandon that fantasy, combined with new-found knowledge that I am actually a coward and could never handle being in any danger zone), I met real live female foreign reporters. One day I felt so inadequate telling them I was writing articles for airline magazines that I wanted to slide under the lunch table. Since I was extremely pregnant at the time, it was a physical impossibility, but I would gladly have disappeared by magic if I had been capable.

Self-confidence and self-esteem have to be nurtured slowly and deliberately. The first time you go out and do something by yourself, you gain both confidence in your abilities to function in a new city and a better feeling about yourself. The trick is to attempt something relatively easy, thereby guaranteeing success. I am not making this up: on our second posting, just the simple act of successfully purchasing a box of paper clips in a downtown Taipei stationery store boosted my morale enormously (to say nothing of my skills at charades). Take small steps at first.

It can be very difficult for even the most energetic of souls to project an identity separate from her husband's when settling into a posting. After all, his job is still the main event no matter how busy you get. He has all the instant status. Yours will come in time. So in the beginning, accept that you are Mrs. Husband's Job for now, and be patient for the return of your own credibility as an individual. What is important is that *you* know who you are, not some stranger you may never see again in your life. I realize this is easier said than done, but it is a terrific character building exercise to begin measuring your self-worth in your own eyes rather than in someone else's. Returning home with that ability under your belt will also be a lot more useful than some trinket you will have to dust every second day.

If you have kept your maiden name rather than taken your husband's, now is *not* the time to change it. Keep your own name. Some women revert to married names overseas because they think it is simpler to explain who they are. The quickest way to lose your own identity is to give up the name you have been using for the past number of decades. In many countries, it is the custom for women to keep their maiden names, so you would not be that unusual. And sometimes, last names get lost in the shuffle anyway. For most of my first posting in Thailand, I was known as Mrs. Robin (or a close approximation), so switching to a married name would have served no purpose, except to fuel my identity crisis.

One last comment about identities: print up name cards for yourself which do not mention your spouse. Not only are name cards a great way to get home in a taxi (if you have the card printed in the local language on one side), but they are also proof positive that you exist outside of your marriage, at least in print.

And Speaking Of Your Marriage

The dynamics of your marriage may very well change when you move overseas, and you will find yourself simultaneously adapting to a new country and a new role as spouse that you did not play at home. Not only will the host country view you in a completely different light from what you may be used to, but your spouse may also suddenly heap expectations upon you that were not part of your original nuptial agreement.

If you are the wife of a businessman or diplomat who is expected to host a lot of official entertainments, you may suddenly be playing chatelaine of a large household and staff, organizing cocktail receptions or sit-down dinner parties for twelve. If you are married to a foreign aid worker, you could be thrust into life in poverty-stricken villages in which your spouse expects you to organize a women's weaving co-operative. While some women find such opportunities challenging, not everyone is suited for these activities, and arguments over just what is expected of you as Mrs. Whatever Organization could get heated.

Likewise, childcare responsibilities, which may have been egalitarian at home, may change when you move to a foreign country. The husband may be expected to "officially" play golf on Saturday and Sunday mornings, leaving you to entertain the children for the day. Or in the presence of so many household helpers, the working partner may suddenly decide to flee the home since help is on the scene, despite your pleas that a maid is not a parent. Likewise, a husband who used to help back home may fail to notice that the wife he just transplanted into a Western society where the price of household help is exorbitant is looking pretty weary from her new unasked-for role as a nanny and housekeeper.

Further disagreements can break out if you decide to work and your new job interferes with your spouse's. After all, you may very well be reminded in no uncertain terms, you have not moved thousands of miles for *your* job. Seething resentment will lie behind your smile (if you are still capable of one) while you attempt to cancel your plans or rearrange your life to reach a so-called compromise definitely not in your favour. Or perhaps you have not worked since the children were born, and suddenly your husband, thrust into a Western society that necessitates two incomes, is hinting none too subtly about you getting a part-time job, forgetting that someone has to be around for the children, especially if he is on the road most of the time.

Expectations of just what will be required of you overseas must be hammered out before you leave home and then renegotiated regularly once you are living abroad. Keep the lines of communication open and honest. I told my diplomat husband that under no circumstances would I go to cocktail parties unless they were of particular interest to me. For one thing, they are fattening (especially when you glue yourself to the food table), and for another, I hate getting all dressed up for any occasion. So over the years, my husband and I reached an agreement that satisfied my waistline and my ego. I rarely went to official functions.

If you do plan to work, parameters must be set up with your spouse and your employer to avoid disputes. You cannot maintain any credibility if you take the responsibilities of a job only to inform your employer that your spouse feels a dinner party has to take precedence over an assigned job task. The credibility of working accompanying spouses is already stretched in some foreign communities, and you ruin it for serious professional women if you must rush home from work in order to oversee the preparation of hors d'oeuvres.

Like many other aspects of living abroad, extra effort must be put into marriage because there are tensions and circumstances that can be very different from home. The ladies of the British Raj, for instance, very often found themselves married to men who suddenly went from modest, humble fellows back home in England to self-important, aggrandizing, obnoxious chaps overseas (and these may have been only men low on the Raj totem pole). Hard evidence suggests some things have not changed much since colonial service. Be on the lookout for inflated egos so that everyone's feet can remain firmly on the ground.

Delicate Conditions and Hypochondria

World health conditions have improved, but it is still true that you could occasionally pick up some rare disease when you move abroad. More often, however, spouses fall victim to a side effect of "nothing to do" syndrome, one certainly well documented by the ladies of the Raj. That is, the collapse of otherwise hearty women into delicate creatures.

Admittedly, women of the nineteenth century were not expected to appear as sturdy as they actually were, but an account in an 1830 journal by one woman noted that "most Englishwomen in India in the Early Raj days had entirely given up walking. They rode on horseback or were carried about in palanquins."

Before you dismiss such laziness as a condition of an earlier century, consider there may be a twenty-first-century replacement in many overseas posts: the driver. Having lived in busy, congested cities where complete anarchy reigns in traffic and driving yourself around is admittedly suicidal, I still believe that driver lethargy is a condition that befalls many an accompanying spouse. What should be used as a convenience (for grocery shopping, picking up children from school, navigating difficult districts) can quickly become a replacement for using your own two legs to walk two feet to buy milk. A new city becomes familiar and more interesting from the ground level. So, even with a driver in your employ, walking to where you need to go should be considered occasionally to keep the body and mind not only healthier, but rooted in the real world as well.

Unnecessary medical appointments, while certainly providing something to do, can get tedious after a while, to say nothing of costly. Before you leave home, make sure you are healthy enough to live abroad, and save yourself the trouble of moving if you are not. At the same time, do not be alarmed if you feel like you are falling apart in small ways when you are first settling in. It is natural to react in non-life-threatening ways to new food, a new lifestyle, and new smells. You are not going crazy. Your body will gain equilibrium after a while and let you function again as a normal human being.

Culture Aftershocks

Many of those small non-debilitating illnesses may also be a result of the second stage of culture shock mentioned in chapter 3. Once you get past the honeymoon phase (where you think everything is marvellous about your new environment), your mood may come tumbling down into complete hostility towards all that surrounds you. When you are in such a frame of mind, it is not surprising that your body may react in subtle and not-so-subtle ways.

Fear of your new environment, which may not have been that strong upon arrival, may grow when you realize that you are in fact staying and not returning home as if on a vacation. Traffic, dirty streets, or anything that may have seemed quaint at the beginning suddenly becomes impossible to bear a minute longer, or frightens you from stepping out into the street. It becomes a case less of having nothing to do and more of being afraid to do anything at all. Many of these fears are also symptoms of culture shock and will disappear after a while like every other phase associated with your move abroad.

So What Do I Do?

It is hard to get someone else motivated, but I can offer some of the strategies I have used on myself that work.

Make yourself at home

When it finally sinks in that wherever you are, you will likely be staying for a while, you can do yourself a big favour and start feeling like you *are* at home, not in some transitory place. There is no greater impediment to getting on with things than feeling like you will only be somewhere for a short time, so why should you bother getting anything started? Instead, get used to your new digs as quickly as possible. Tell yourself that you are finished puttering around with interior decorating and essential errands. When you feel that something is unfinished, it can get in the way of moving on to the next project. So go ahead, pick up your purse and go out the door. Join the local library, volunteer somewhere, take up yoga or tai chi, register for an aerobics class, go for that facial, *get on* with your new life.

Homesickness can be counterproductive

Sure, it would be nice to be in your home country for a variety of reasons, but you are not there, and the sooner you stop acting like Dorothy in *The Wizard of Oz* (chanting "There's no place like home"), the better off you will feel. When I lived in Asia, my heart would ache in September when I knew that the leaves were changing colour back home, while I stared at trees with leaves that never dropped, never mind changed colour. I would try to let the longing wash over me like a nice dream, then wake up and get on with my life at hand. I did not always succeed, but as I tell my daughter, even mothers are not perfect. At least I tried. You should too.

Set priorities on your time

When you have difficulties getting started with your new routine, it can often be due to an overwhelming sense of time commitments to spouse, children, volunteer organizations, and then finally, yourself. In some foreign settings, time becomes fractured due to schedules compounded by the level of difficulty in navigating the city. On our second posting in Taiwan, for instance, traffic congestion made a trip into the downtown area from the expatriate district at least a three-hour affair (leaving about twenty minutes for whatever I was trying to do). Because my children were young at the time, and I was on duty every few hours for a pickup or delivery, I rarely saw the inner city.

If you find yourself in such circumstances, one positive step to get over feeling distracted by a fractured time frame is to sit down and figure out how much time you want, or need, to give to all the activities critical in your life. Do not be dismayed if you find personal time limited to only twenty- or thirty-minute stretches. It is amazing what one can do despite time constraints.

Get your mind off yourself

Stop worrying about things you cannot change. In this instance, I do not only mean your new environment. I mean your body, your unruly hair, even your personality. Focus outward and look around you rather than becoming self-absorbed, which I know is extraordinarily difficult to do when you are feeling sorry for yourself. If you want to change something, think about going after that which you can change, like your skills, or your knowledge about your host culture.

Two Roads Diverged

When you move abroad, you are presented with two fundamental choices. You can choose to be either a cool spectator or an active participant in your new culture. The latter option does not necessarily have to mean studying hundreds of hours to become fluent in a foreign tongue or going native completely. It could simply mean not sitting on the sidelines (or in a rented apartment) and wasting a golden opportunity that you will most certainly later regret.

Not everyone will start a lucrative business or begin a new career when they live overseas. But most people do have the capability of walking out their door and opening their eyes to soak in the colours, rhythms, customs, even just the street life of a foreign city. If you think there is nothing to do, think again.

5 Careers Can Travel Too
Success Depends on Your State of Mind

My friends may find it hard to believe this, but I eventually did calm down considerably when contemplating the notion of working abroad. After a certain point, my pulse no longer quickened, my patience did not fly out the window, and my self-esteem in general did not automatically plummet when I considered that great philosophical query known to most travelling wives: "What the hell am I going to do over there and can I make any money from it?"

That is not to say that I abandoned altogether my ornery harangues of officials of any stripe who could possibly employ wives overseas or lobby for more moral support from my own government's foreign outposts. I made a career out of it, actually. Talk about the irony of life! Any corporate human resources person who has heard me speak these past twenty years can testify that I can still work up a passionate sweat and go into my strident spouse routine on cue. But somewhere along the line, and I hate to admit that age and motherhood may actually have had something to do with it, I gradually changed what I previously had perceived as the rewards of an organized, linear working life. In other words, I did some serious rethinking about what a "career" should really mean in the context of a mobile life.

What Exactly Is a Career?
How you define the word "career" in your own mind can make or break you. If you believe the word "career" should include such notions as moving up a corporate ladder, pay raises, promotions, or even mentors, stop right there. As a travelling wife,

the popular interpretation of the word "career" is just out of sync with your life on the move. The structure necessary to promote those concepts just will not be there. Your professional life is quite unique.

Consider instead a more appropriate definition of the word "career," one that actually comes out of a dictionary—to prove I am not making this up to make you feel better. I found one such definition of the word "career" to mean "a path through life."

When applied to women, travelling or not, this definition makes infinitely more sense. For on a path, there are no corporate checkpoints, no great rush. You can amble along, let people pass you by if they are in a hurry, or just stroll off the main path to see what lies down another winding trail. You can stop along a path; it may change in scenery and terrain, but no matter where you are in the world, it's still *your* path and not somebody else's. You are your own judge. There are no lifestyle writers hiding in the bushes waiting to jump out and chronicle your experiences for the women's pages. You alone gauge the distance you want to go.

What Is a Mobile Career?

A mobile career is your own path, one you can jump onto anywhere in the world and feel at home. You set your own pace, and most important of all, you use all the talents that make you unique. When you see the path as one for an entire life and not merely a short stop until the next promotion, you are not limiting yourself to one vocation. Everything you do will become part of your career: from raising children to foreign travel to working at a variety of jobs.

Instead of presuming that moving abroad means you are giving up the skills you trained for, recognize that on a lifelong career path you will not only pick up new skills, but also discover ones you never suspected you had. In a mobile career, different skills become useful at different times. Your options are *limitless*, not limited.

Working outside of a structure also gives you more flexibility. You can accommodate distractions peculiar to overseas life like home leave, exotic holidays, or visitors from home. The only obstacles to a successful mobile career in these newly defined terms are inapplicable expectations.

Adjusting Your Career Expectations and Values

Ask yourself what constitutes a successful career. Is it money? Prestige? Having a high profile? Once again, in a travelling life, these values may simply not apply, so why bother torturing yourself trying to achieve the impossible?

Materialistic measuring sticks, like money, are often so inappropriate on a foreign posting and especially if you are posted to a developing country, where you will likely begin to view materialism in a new light. I do not advocate working for nothing. If you are a professional, you should be paid something. But if a job appeals to you, do not turn it down because the pay is not what you expected it to be. Try to determine new ways of measuring and evaluating success that are appropriate to your new travelling life, and also to the stage and experience you have reached in living overseas.

On the first time out, you may need to find out what you are capable of doing. Your experience may be limited, so you may not be able to accomplish all that you want to do. On our first time abroad, I simply was not ready for my fantasy of foreign reporting. I was not only a neophyte in Asia, incapable of differentiating the warring factions in nearby Cambodia, I was also at the age when the idea of childbearing was most appealing.

Timing can be critical but this is often a lesson you learn the hard way. It would have been unrealistic for me to expect to run out and try to join *Time* magazine when I lived in Bangkok but that is practically what I did, not only during our first year overseas, but in my seventh month of pregnancy. I had panicked over my professional life, and upon hearing that *Time* might

CAREERS CAN TRAVEL TOO

have needed a new stringer to work with the Bangkok-based correspondent, I foolishly made an appointment to meet him.

After walking over to the correspondent's home and miscalculating the distance, I stood before him, my résumé and clippings limp in my hand from the humidity, watching his face evaluate and try to understand why the sweaty, bloated blob of a woman standing before him could conceivably want freelance work at such an advanced state of pregnancy. He obviously had not met many compulsive travelling female careerists.

If he had, he might have done a story about them. Still, I will always give the man credit for some compassion, because he started telling me about the birth of his own Bangkok baby instead of completely humiliating me on the spot. And needless to say, he told me to come back after I had had the baby and we would talk more comfortably then. I never set my eyes on him again.

So what is my advice? Go ahead and act as if you were a person possessed, about your career anyways. Try everything. Be rejected. Be disappointed. It truly does build character and helps you out in the long run. This advice is not intended to sound patronizing, because it is obviously coming from a formerly possessed person. But sometimes it does not hurt to get some things out of your system.

When I returned home from my "interview" with *Time,* I went to bed and would not come out for two days. In the end, though, I was able to laugh at myself about it, and to use the experience to remind myself that sometimes, it pays to wait.

How Do I Spell Success? Not M*O*N*E*Y

Here is an exercise I devised for myself to help me develop a healthier (and happier) professional perspective on moving abroad. When we were posted back to Canada after three years in Bangkok, I abandoned mainstream journalism for the most part and switched over to selling my various communications skills. This meant I could work for a variety of people as either a scriptwriter or speechwriter, audiovisual producer or propaganda writer, communications strategist or any other lofty title I decided to assign myself.

Was I successful? That depends entirely on what I consider qualifies as "success." In some of my work, notably my lucrative consultant's contracts from the Canadian government, I will confess that money made me feel quite successful. More important to me was achieving a working life that combined the flexibility and balance of working from home and having children. Unconsciously, I was desperately seeking work-life balance before it became fashionable.

Upon hearing that we would be moving once again to Asia for several years, once again forcing me to not only start the process of building new contacts but also lose a substantial income, I admit I momentarily slipped into that horrible state of Total Despair that many women are familiar with. The time had clearly arrived for a personal re-evaluation and reassessment of the meaning of "success" vis-à-vis happiness abroad.

In my view, the primary lesson I needed to learn to keep my sanity was how to teach myself to get away from viewing success in my crass, materialistic Western way: money. So I put this question to myself: Why will a major cut in pay actually be an advantage to me both personally and professionally? To my own surprise, I came up with several positive and satisfying answers by listing previously unarticulated, non-materialistic bonuses to life abroad.

I may take a pay cut, I told myself, but in return I will gain the following benefits:

- Adventure, travel, exotica
- The opportunity to be creative (to write something other than government bafflegab)
- An escape route from government bureaucracy and petty officials

- Enormous amounts of quality family time
- Cultural exposure and lessons of tolerance (which would also be terrific for my children)
- Experience that might not translate into a job right away but would come in handy at a later date

Ask Yourself Why You Want to Work Overseas

Aside from money, which we would all love to make, it is important to truly understand your motives for wanting to seek work abroad. They will ultimately affect the decisions you make about the kind of work to pursue or accept.

If you set intellectual stimulation to keep from going crazy as your goal (the choice I tended to choose overseas), your chances of success are considerably greater. Why? You broaden your options and chances of success. So many projects overseas can be stimulating by virtue of their novelty. It may only take one small, part-time project to succeed if intellectual excitement is your goal. This is not measured by a paycheque; it can be obtained by meeting people or by reading material; it can be self-initiated; and very often it can be done from home with a limited number of childcare arrangements if your children are still young. It also provides an answer to that dreaded of all questions occasionally asked of a spouse: "And what do you do?"

'I Gave Up My Career for You!'

Probably the worst philosophical argument which runs through the mind of a woman on a posting is that she has not only given up her career to be with her husband, but she has also given up the status and recognition that went with her profession. Before you can move onto the job of finding a job, you must first grapple with this identity crisis, which many women before you have had to come to terms with. This issue goes beyond the idea of making money and is really about respect. We all want it, and often it takes a job to feel like we are getting enough of it.

There is no surefire advice I can offer a woman in the throes of this issue. Like flying long-distance or unpacking endless boxes of kitchen gadgets, this is simply one that has to be endured. Finding a job or any situation that makes you feel happy and normal again will naturally help your ego return to a state you can live with. Until that day arrives, though, many women will find it hard to keep their emotions from jumping all over the place. For some, those emotions will hit rock bottom. In this instance, it helps to talk to as many women as possible, if only to reassure yourself that you are not the first to go through this experience. It is a facet of moving abroad that will never go away easily. Just let it run its course.

Motivation: Do Not Leave Home Without It

We all need to have our dreams. But remember that nothing, absolutely nothing, will happen to you overseas unless you personally make it happen. You must be willing to be a little bit afraid, to step outside your comfort zone. There are going to be risks to working in a foreign environment, not the least of which will be a morbid fear of getting lost on the way to your interview.

Not everyone has the same level of adrenalin, courage, *chutzpah,* or sheer foolhardiness, but everyone has a little. You have agreed to move overseas, haven't you? Some of your friends back home are likely already telling you they are in awe of your nerve.

Sitting in your new overseas home will not get you a job unless you are actively using the phone or the Internet to find one. Eventually, you will have to go outside your door to look for work, because nobody is going to hand you some nicely organized, structured nine-to-five job. In foreign communities where such aberrations do exist, you will find yourself competing with hundreds of other spouses for the privilege of holding such a job.

All the skills in the world are useless to you unless you are motivated enough to pick up the phone, or send that e-mail, or seek out that individual whose name you were given by someone you do not know but whose son plays with your daughter. If you think anyone is going to hand you something, especially your husband's employer, you will be sorely disappointed.

The pressure to succeed and the feeling that finding a job is the only way to make your new life bearable have a tremendous effect on your level of motivation. They will spur you into action. If aggressive behaviour is frowned upon back in your own culture, you will surprise yourself at how quickly you will adapt to the ways of your host culture. When you truly want to find work, your adrenalin will start pumping. I have seen this over and over again among women from all sorts of different cultures and could write an entire book filled with success stories of women who have reinvented their professional lives.

Never Agree to Anything Before You Get There

Never, ever agree to any job until you see your new home, city, country, environment, or the lay of the land. I have seen women run around half possessed, lining up work for their posting from home with companies, governments, schools, and other likely employers. They sign on the dotted line before they have any idea what their schedules will be like over there. They do not know whether they will have transportation or how bad traffic can be, what wages might be, and so on. You can guess what I am getting at here. It may make a great story to hear some wife tell you about how she started work the instant she arrived at post, but read between the lines. Those would be the stress lines all over her face.

When we moved to Bangkok, the thought of being idle for even one minute depressed me. I instantly ran out and lined up a job doing what many expatriate wives desperate for work end up doing, teaching English. That is perfect for someone with

ESL training or teaching experience in general. But for a journalist like me, it was horrible. I hated it immediately and had to plot for four months afterwards how to get out of my commitment.

Yes, it would be nice to know in advance what you may do *over there,* but give yourself time to unpack your boxes and figure out which end is up before plunging into work. Certainly explore possibilities with potential employers, but wait until the culture shock fog lifts from your head before racing across town in traffic to a job you are not sure you even want.

You may also need the time to set up childcare arrangements that satisfy everyone concerned. When your children are in school all day, it becomes a little easier to arrange time to work. If they are preschoolers, it could take a few months to sort out childcare, activities, and other related duties. I have worked from home my entire married life and firmly believe, for me anyway, it was one of the best choices I have ever made not only for my family but for me personally. It certainly is one of the best options when your children are still young (or you are still producing them).

Living in a developing country where household help is an affordable option, you can combine motherhood and work by assigning yourself a work area and teaching your children early on to respect your space. Of course, it takes a bit of discipline to work from home, but consider the fringe benefits: you can still be there when they come home from school or wake up from their nap. And you are not stuck in an office all day worrying how you will get the laundry or grocery shopping done. It can all be squeezed in with a little time management and, of course, a supportive husband.

Know What Your Skills Are

It also does not hurt to have an inventory of your own skills. This is definitely something you can begin to put together before leaving home and finish off in the early days after your arrival overseas. Résumés, while useful, are never enough because they often do not reveal the full extent of your skills.

Since I first wrote this book, the sheer volume of new career-related resources online or in print has been mind-boggling. (See the resources section for my favourites.) The career bible when I first wrote this, and it remains so to this day, is *What Color Is Your Parachute?* by Richard Bolles, which now has a website to accompany it at jobhuntersbible.com. Author Bolles divides skills into three main areas: skills with people (including animals), skills with information, and skills with things.

Skills that involve people and information are particularly useful for people on the move and never more so than in the wireless world. Some of the skills involving people, according to Bolles, include working with animals, training, counselling, advising and consulting, treating, founding and leading, negotiating and deciding, managing and supervising, performing and amusing, persuading, communicating, sensing, feeling, serving, and finally, taking instructions.

Skills with information include achieving, expediting, planning and developing, designing, creating, synthesizing, improving, adapting, visualizing, evaluating, organizing, analyzing, researching, computing, copying, storing, retrieving, comparing, and observing. Using those suggestions, try making a list of your own skills. The website will also help you with online career tests.

It Takes More Than Skills: Be Creative

I have already mentioned that motivation is essential to a satisfying professional life overseas. Now add to that a large dose of creativity. In most cases abroad, you must create your own opportunities and market your own skills. You must dream up creative ways of selling yourself. Admittedly, it often takes an outsider to see the possibilities for someone else.

I was having lunch one day in Taipei with a newly arrived nurse who told me she was especially interested in herbal, holistic medicine. We were chatting about Chinese natural medicines when she told me she had met a Chinese doctor who had actually expressed an interest in her working for him, in his pharmacy no less, on a part-time basis. She could not quite decide what to do. So I offered the suggestion that she negotiate something part-time in order to learn from this doctor about Chinese medicines, which information in my view, when compiled, would make a great handbook for the foreigners of Taipei. I know she went out to see the doctor the next day, and while some perfect scenario may not have come of it right away, she was beginning to see that there were possibilities with a little bit of creativity.

In Beijing, I met each week with three other women with whom I had formed an ad hoc support group. We sat around drinking too many cups of coffee, listening and evaluating each other's ideas for working. There does not have to be a common theme to your work fantasies either: my support group consisted of one former Taiwanese journalist, one Harvard-educated environmental lawyer, one budding self-help book writer (guess who), and one entrepreneurial free spirit who beat all of us to the marketplace with Chinese peasant painting T-shirts, which sold like hotcakes by her first Christmas in Beijing.

Not only has the Internet allowed expats to stay in touch with one another, it has been a boon for spouses wishing to pursue careers overseas or stay in touch or up to date with the one they left behind. So work the Internet.

Focus, Focus, Focus

Let me share a lesson I learned as a freelance journalist. When I would approach a publication I was anxious to write for, I learned very quickly that it was not enough for me to simply inform an editor that I would like to write for his magazine. *Write what?* the editor would wonder, before filing my letter in the nearest wastebasket. Instead, I learned to write "query" letters that made specific story suggestions, and usually not just one but several.

In other words, after reading a magazine I wanted to write for (another lesson, know your market or the organization you are approaching), I would suggest an article idea that I knew fit a publication. *I did my homework.* Naturally, we all do not know exactly what we want to do, but having some ideas worked out (a simple "I'd like to work with children" may yield leads) will prove invaluable to you when you meet someone and investigate the possibilities of plugging into a project. The key to someone hiring you is learning to make your case so that someone decides (a) they need the certain kind of service for their business or organization that you are offering; and (b) you, and nobody else, are the person to provide that service.

Prepare Your Own Personal Marketing Strategy

Imagine this. A former top management consultant, executive, or simply intelligent woman is going overseas for the first time with her husband. At home, that individual worked for years managing several employees, overseeing expensive administrative budgets, or designing and implementing complicated projects of any description. The individual was known to be cool under pressure, strong in her judgment skills, and confident of her own abilities.

Someone asks her what she will do overseas, and despair, confusion, or a combination of both crosses her face. She is at a temporary loss. So this individual is asked: Why not apply all those management skills to yourself? Instead of planning a megaproject, plan your own employment future using the same variables. Context, goals, roles of various players, time constraints, budget considerations, deadlines, target audience, marketing potential, and voilà, a business idea may be born.

Your Husband's Organization: Stay Clear

How can I put this nicely? I can't, so let me use a comparison. My advice on travelling on airplanes with small children always points out that some flight attendants tend to treat you as something akin to a leper. Sure, they are supposed to offer assistance, hand out toys, or guarantee certain seating, but I advise people never to count on anything. If a flight crew is nice and helpful, think of it as a bonus.

The same principle applies to your husband's organization, whether it is a bank, a government, or a small business venture. If there are individuals ready to hire spouses, ready to think of a spouse in terms of her professional skills rather than merely the expensive luggage accompanying the employee, consider yourself lucky.

It is usually against a company's policy to hire a spouse over-seas for all sorts of trumped-up reasons: conflict of interest, husband and wife teams won't work, you get the picture. In some cases, it is the top-ranking official's wife who does not want to see another wife in the office full-time. I am not being bitchy, either. I have seen a lot of that.

If you feel like trying your luck, though, here is a piece of advice. When you switch hats from accompanying spouse to professional, *be professional.* Arrange meetings during office hours, with résumés and proposals. State your objectives and pay expectations or working hours clearly. Do not drop into the office with a child in tow to chat about business or hit someone up for a job at a party. If you want to be treated like a professional, act like one.

But make sure you have enough medication to counter high blood pressure, because take it from someone who knows: It can be a sucker's game.

Stick to Outside Targets

Universities, institutions, relocation companies, and non-governmental organizations are often good hiring grounds. Likewise, multilateral organizations such as the United Nations or World Bank often hire locally. International offices or chambers of commerce are also worth a gambit. International schools recruit primarily from abroad but still have local hires on staff.

Never pass by a bulletin board anywhere without stopping. Start with what you know best. That is, a health care worker should approach hospitals, musician approach music schools, and so on. Instead of just trying to answer newspaper employment advertisements in the English-language press or on a local website, try placing one about yourself.

The 'Hassle Factor'

After a few personal work experiences that left me wrung out emotionally, I developed a litmus test to assess what I used to call the "hassle factor" of any potential job, and not just overseas. First things first: no matter how straightforward a project may sound, absolutely nothing is easy in a country that is foreign to you. People never do business the same way you do back home, so always be prepared to learn a few cross-cultural lessons along the way.

You may accept a job or contract and only later discover that it is a complicated process just to find the people you need to see, interview, or meet. They may have no phone, or their office is two bus rides away. If you are a Westerner, a potential employer may assume you have a driver. Or how about this: you are hired to do one job only to find out that in actual fact, they would like you to do ten others, and will call you at all hours with more requests or want up-to-the-minute progress reports.

Language is another hassle factor, as very often the English spoken in the host country does not sound like the English you know. One day, I got a call out of the blue from an editor associated with the American Medical Association. Would I be interested in attending a medical convention being held in Bangkok? All I would have to do, it was explained to me, was take notes of the proceedings. *Easy enough,* I thought, without thinking it through.

The esteemed doctors had gathered in a local five-star hotel. Although I did not recognize any names, it sure looked impressive to me. And then the first speaker addressed the gathering. I leaned forward to hear better because it sounded like a foreign language. No. It was English. Except English was so obviously not this particular doctor's mother tongue, nor was it the first language of the second, third, and fourth speakers on the program. They were making valiant efforts and so was I, until I was as white as the paper on my lap. There was no way I could understand a single word, never mind the complicated medical jargon they were using. I had to quit, something I hate to do after making a commitment.

Consider every potential assignment very carefully. Ask yourself a few questions: Where will you be working? Will you be paid in this century? Will you have to bargain for your fee? (I had to once, unexpectedly, with a Thai cabinet minister I was writing English speeches for. Not the job, incidentally, I had been hired to do.)

The Importance of Networking

In the overseas context, networking is not just connecting for you. It is helping others network too, because at this particular juncture in your working life, cutthroat competition, back-stabbing, and office politics are themes that are not only inappropriate, they are counterproductive as well. Overseas, you have to be a lot nicer.

Sound crazy? Not when you consider how important support groups become when you move abroad. From mothers' organizations to addiction groups to groups of women who like to sew but cannot find the right materials, women find they need each other a lot more than they might at home. It is true we all know a few women we would like to throw out a window, but when you stop and give every woman the benefit of the doubt, you will find it takes you a lot further in your relationships overseas.

When you live far away from home and need to make friends and connections, you will not get very far by being a pill. You need to rediscover your basic nicer self in the absence of that hype and competition back home that may have thrown you off balance too much of the time, making you act too often in your own, and only your own, interest.

That kind of strategy just will not work overseas because it is difficult to operate in a vacuum. So, when hearing or asking about different jobs, think about whether you know someone else who may fit the bill if a particular job is not for you. What goes around comes around, or so the saying goes. You can help yourself by helping others in the work game—and discover a few joys of friendship in the bargain. The women in the support group I was part of in Beijing, not surprisingly, became my best friends.

You Will Come Home Again

Allow me to return again to my metaphor for "career" as a path through life. That path, despite all its detours, may eventually take you home again, so it is wise to plan ahead for what may lie down the road. This can be accomplished by asking a few basic questions: Can I do this back home? When at home, ask it in reverse: Can I do this while I am away?

I was lucky to have writing skills, which can transfer easily with a lot of self-discipline, but mine are not the only ones that can be mobile. In particular, here are a few other portable ideas: anything that can be done from home on a self-employment basis, such as computer skills, accounting, editing, creative pursuits, public relations, photography, small business ventures, catering, management consulting, briefing or coaching other expatriates about adaptation, or being the point person for visiting delegations of anything.

Outside the home, consider the health care industry, teaching, social services like counselling, office management, international development, English as a second language, private tutoring, fundraising, museum and art gallery functions, and the hotel and travel industries.

Be True to Yourself

Above all else, do not change professions to keep up with your husband. When my husband went into the foreign service, some friends asked me if I would too. Are you kidding me? *Me, a diplomat?* Never mind that I could have been laughed out of the examination room of the diplomatic service exams. (I once wrote the aptitude tests for law school and thought my results would tell me I have the intelligence of a fly.) I reminded my friends that I was a journalist and a writer. If my husband wanted to learn to speak Chinese, that was his business. I would stick to just eating Chinese food.

So my final word on this subject is this: try to go after something professional that offers mobility, but in all cases be true to your own talents and your own dreams. If you are happy doing your own thing, following your own unique path in life wherever it may take you, you can be happy wherever you are in the world.

6 Maids and Madams
The Mixed Blessing of Household Help

The mixed blessing of household helpers is simple: they are there when you want them, but also when you *don't* want them.

How could I possibly not want them? I wondered when briefed about live-in help before going on our first assignment. How could I not want someone around who was prepared to wash my clothes every day? Iron my husband's shirts? Change dirty diapers on my future babies? Cook for me every night? I knew it sounded too good to be true, but could the downside of such full-time assistance with my life really be that terrible? The person briefing me, a professional travelling wife of many years' experience, just smiled and said, "Wait. You'll see it's not all a bed of roses."

It took me less than two days to discover the thorn. The first day was terrific. We had just arrived at our Bangkok apartment when a Thai maid took the groceries from my hand, disappeared into the kitchen, and shortly after placed a delicious platter of Thai rice before us for lunch. Our shipment had not even arrived yet with our dishes and pots and pans, but "Madam," as I was to be known during my stay in Thailand, did not have to bother anymore with such trivial matters. I was just to sit back and enjoy.

The next morning at dawn, when "Master" went off to report to the embassy (which opened at 7 a.m.) and "Madam" was depressed out of her mind because a long day of nothing lay ahead, I discovered my Thai maid had made my bed before I could crawl back into it. Then, while I sat staring into space on the living-room couch, she was staring blankly at me while she vacuumed around my feet before setting off to the market to buy my food. I was becoming more suicidal by the second at the thought of a full-time audience for my mood swings, to say nothing of the guilt I felt from watching her do everything I hated to do myself, in return for a slave wage scale. The scene pushed my guilt barometer over the edge. Household help was not just going to be a mixed blessing, I cried to myself. It was going to be a curse.

The Culture Shock of Household Help

I had read enough trashy novels with an exotic Asian setting to recognize what was happening to me, but I had been temporarily distracted by the exhaustion of jet lag. Like other newcomers to the developing world, I was suffering from the shock of moving to a culture at a time when the labour supply was abundant, and anybody, certainly not just the privileged, could have a houseful of people looking after them for an extremely low price.

If you have never allowed anyone other than a cleaning service or your mother to see your messy closet, you may be in for a shock the first time you return home and find a maid, amah, *ayi*, houseboy, nanny, helper, whoever ironing your husband's underwear. After the blush dies down on your face (especially if it is not even your maid doing the ironing, but a visiting friend of hers, which was the case for me), you will begin to feel guilty for making her do all the dirty work you do not want to do, such as ironing, cleaning vegetables, or straightening up your children's toys. You will wonder how she can stay so good-natured considering how little you are paying her.

All of these doubts come with the culture shock of having household help, which can really hit you in the face the first time you experience it. It is a condition only expatriates and especially those from developed countries who move to developing countries can understand. Back home you may have had help, but you paid through the nose for it. In some overseas settings, people come and go in your house or apartment and are clearly in charge of areas of responsibility you once called your own: your children, your cupboards and pantry. Suddenly, you feel like your status has been elevated as high as a character in *Masterpiece Theatre*, except that this is not some nineteenth-century television drama. On the other hand, expatriates from some developing countries used to having household help suddenly find they have to do everything for themselves when they move to a Western country, and that can be equally disconcerting.

One way a woman can gauge whether she is reacting to the idea of having help for the first time in her life (and mothers do not count) is the sudden onslaught of a mixture of good and evil thoughts running frantically through her mind. That is, at the same time that she is guilt-ridden, she is also secretly thrilled every time the maid calls her "Madam," "Memsahib," or, my favourite honorific while living in Taipei, "Missy." The guilt phase quickly passes and before you know it, you are being waited on like everyone else. Worse still, you are likely bitching to your friends that your maid shows no initiative, needs to be shown how to do things, or her culinary skills (despite being a whiz at the local food) are just not up to scratch. Believe me, you get used to having a household helper, provided you have found a good one.

Hiring Help

I have been thrown into several different situations when it comes to household help. I had the situation I described when we moved to Bangkok, where my maid apparently came with the apartment; the situation where I needed to find help myself; and the worst situation of all, where help was assigned to me with little or no choice on my part. That last option occurred in China back in the early 1990s when the political situation was tricky; it was definitely the worst of all worlds but is a situation that can still have a happy ending, if you are lucky.

In most developing countries you can plug into a network of babysitters. Most amahs or maids in any given city have a group of friends whose names they are ready to provide on request. When you need to hire someone, you simply ask your friend's help if they have a friend in need of a job. If that comes up dry, women's clubs or social organizations usually have bulletin boards with leads, especially as the time you arrive is normally a turnover period for personnel. Someone is bound to be advertising the fact that their help (wonderful with children or not afraid of dogs) is now available. Websites and other Internet-based communities can also be helpful.

Often an embassy or company has a roster of people who have been employed by staff over the years and are used to certain expatriate ways of living. It is not unusual for staff to work for ten years or more for a rotational staff of an organization. These are always the best kind of helpers, for not only will they be loyal and sensitive to your particular ethnic quirks, but they will also likely be able to tell you about all the people who have served in your company or embassy for the past decade. Remember though, every time your maid tells a story about a previous employer, that you will be the next topic of conversation when you leave.

Who to Hire

When we arrived in Taipei on our second posting, with a two-year-old with us, I hired our amah even before we had left the hotel for our permanent quarters. We had plugged into the amah network early and were fortunate to have a gem of a woman sent over immediately to meet us. Of course, I did not know she was a gem at the time, but it helped when she pulled out of her purse a photo album showing multiple pictures of the children she had looked after for the past thirty years. I knew I was meeting a pro.

I was so anxious to get out for a few hours, alone with Rodney, I decided that unless I took an instant dislike to the woman, I would bolt the minute my kids seemed comfortable. Luckily for us, I liked her immediately and my first impression turned out to be correct. We went out for a short two-hour supper at a nearby restaurant, informed the hotel staff that a new amah was in the room, and enjoyed our first peaceful meal in about three weeks.

Of course, we were taking a chance, but when someone comes recommended and you get a good feeling about her, as we did (which was especially reinforced when we returned from supper to find she had cleaned up our hotel room), you can only hope for the best. Some people will never leave their children alone. They transfer all their own fears to them and only later wonder why their children are afraid to be left with a sitter.

I am not recommending that you hire just anyone, but childcare is like a lot of things overseas (medical care, for instance): you simply have to go on faith that everything will turn out all right. We would all like to have a relative nearby, but that is next to impossible overseas, so unless you want to be trapped with your kids for the next few years, cross your fingers and hope for the best. And rely on your own intuition about people. Besides, it is like hiring someone at home. If they do not work out, you give them notice and you dismiss them.

How to Interview

If you are assigned to a foreign country that has a difficult language you know you will never in a million years and countless survival courses master, conduct the job interview in English. If the person responds in anything remotely understandable to you, give them ten points. Language barriers, if your own skills are limited, can be a pain for three years unless you are a former world champion at charades.

In Beijing, our help was assigned by a government bureau so the interview could not be conducted in English except through a translator. Subsequent communication, I discovered after hiring both cook and maid (known as *ayi*), can actually be carried out through facial expressions, raised eyebrows, lots of pointing, and sharing duty-free cigarettes your husband does not know you are smoking. It also helps if your husband speaks the language, as mine did (but of course, he was at the embassy all day).

Regardless of how you conduct the initial meeting, by yourself or with the help of an interpreter, consider it like any other potential employer-employee interview. You need to know expectations of hours, pay, responsibilities, holidays, and skills. And in return, you need to clearly state your requirements. If you will be doing a lot of entertaining, you will need someone with experience with large dinner parties or cocktail receptions. References help, but expatriate turnover often makes it difficult to follow them up. In the case of assigned personnel, like we had in Beijing, it is simply a matter of crossing your fingers and hoping for the best, which when we lived in China meant hoping the government sent a cook who really was a cook and not a driver pretending to be one, which happened to a fellow embassy wife.

The state of your servant's health can also be a critical issue to you, especially if you have young children or are planning a family. Do not be embarrassed to request that a helper have a thorough medical examination. If she does not agree to one, do not hire her unless she is balking due to financial considerations. In that case, if you have a good feeling about the person but just want confirmation with tests, offer to pay. In developing countries, medical tests can be expensive.

In many countries, your household help may not be limited to just maid or laundress. You could be hiring a driver, in which case your interview could take place on a test drive. After all, that is where his skills will be required, so check them out before you go ahead and hire a former kamikaze taxi driver. It also pays to ask a driver what expectations he may have for overtime. Some drivers quit after just a few months because the couple rarely goes out at night, the lucrative hours for a full-time driver.

When hiring a cook, of course you must test him out in the kitchen and at the dinner table. Fortunately, bad cooks are uncovered in a few meals. Very often you have to demonstrate what you want done in the first few weeks.

Live-In Versus Part-Time

Often this question is answered for you in countries where not only your help will live in, but half her living relations as well. This is common in some developing countries, where your quarters may be a rambling villa with living space for many people at the back of your house. I have known people who have never been quite sure just how many people they were actually supporting. When we lived in China, there was similarly no question about live-in status. Help were not even allowed to spend the night, never mind live with us at that time. They were routinely stopped at the gates of our foreign compounds and checked regularly for their credentials.

Some apartments and homes come with so-called maid's quarters, but whoever designed many of them did not have an able-bodied person in mind when considering space. We had a maid's room off our apartment in Bangkok that barely had air in it, but fortunately our maid returned to her own home every night and rarely stayed in it. When we lived in Taipei, the exorbitant price of help and lack of amah's quarters limited us to part-time day help. In Seoul, we had a beautiful spare bedroom with its own bathroom but our maid would not think of using it, opting instead for a very small room she shared with the laundry. This sent my guilt meter over the top but it was her decision.

The amount of time you want your help around will depend on a variety of factors, not the least of which will be your family configuration. With a new baby in a foreign country, you will likely want help available as much as possible. Without children accompanying you, a part-time cleaning person or laundress will be all you require. It also depends on whether your help is in the country legally or not. For instance, when we lived in Taiwan, Filipina maids, many of them of the highest quality, were often working illegally and therefore had to be live-in or run the risk of an immigration roundup.

When you are living in a house, a full-time guard and gardener will also be a necessity. In general, guards should be investigated as thoroughly as possible, because many break-ins do not involve a forced entry thanks to someone already working on the premises who knew when you would be away on vacation or even out for the evening.

The Absence of Privacy

Remember the point about hired help being a mixed blessing? With a household of people looking after you, it can be difficult to ever feel alone in your own home. Someone will always be around, overhearing a conversation and walking in when they should not. A friend of mine, a long-time resident of Bangkok, put it this way: to her, a day without a maid will be the day she can use the bathroom and not have to close the door.

Household helpers will also know everything about you, including the number of times a week you make love with your husband. Do not ask me how they know, they just do. In some countries, like China when we were assigned there, the help was expected to report on our family's activities on a weekly basis. In Thailand, my maid knew I was pregnant before my doctor confirmed it. You cannot have your maid and privacy too, but you can certainly put up barriers for yourself. Close your bedroom door when you do not want to be disturbed during the day. It may seem like Missy is taking a lot of naps, but you really are just creating a bit of space for yourself to quietly read a book without feeling like somebody is watching.

Speaking of Barriers...

Most Westerners cannot help it, but they want everyone to call them by their first name or indulge in other common acts of familiarity. I am the worst offender, but I learned from experience that being overly familiar with people working for you in your own home can be hazardous to your mental health, to say nothing of your bank account.

It is hard not to treat someone living with you in your own home like family, especially if you are used to help being part of the family, but please take my advice: on posting, keep your help at a distance emotionally. That is not to say you are not friendly and sensitive to their needs. It means staying detached.

How to Avoid Being Controlled by a Servant

When my daughter was born in Bangkok, I almost forgot she was truly my daughter and not a child born specifically for the pleasure of my Thai maid. I would return home from doing an errand to find about ten other Thai maids standing around my daughter's crib, paying homage to mine for the perfect sleeping infant.

The worst incident by my reckoning was the day she grabbed a bottle of formula out of my hand, claiming I was handling it wrong. Worse still, I ended that day with an attack of guilt because I made her cry when I went berserk.

Maybe I am not the best person to be handing out advice on this subject, but I obviously acquired some new-found wisdom in my relationship with my Taiwanese amah. Perhaps she was just truly the gem I felt she was, because my husband (who used to dread getting hysterical phone calls from me at his office, sobbing about the help) remarked while we were living there that for the first time in my life, I had help who was not trying to manipulate me.

I could still be nice and caring, but she would go home at the end of the day and I would not take every sulk, sigh, or grunt personally. And neither should you, if you want to have a healthy relationship with your helper.

Post—Household Help Lethargy

After three years in Thailand, my husband and I forgot how to fold clothes and put them away. It was easier to shove everything in the laundry basket so our maid could wash it before putting it away. Now admittedly, Bangkok weather rarely allowed anything to be worn twice, but even so, we would change our clothes constantly without thinking much about laundry. And then we returned home to Canada. After less than two weeks, I had eliminated from our wardrobes everything made of cotton (which would require ironing) and returned to permanent press. We also relearned the skill of picking up after ourselves, washing dishes, and preparing our own meals.

I have already mentioned the legacy of having a driver is that one can forget how to walk. You also tend to forget that the closest you will get back home to a chauffer-driven ride is in a taxi. Try to remember that your true station in life is not the one you are enjoying as an expatriate overseas.

Your Children and Household Help

As hard as I have found it, even with all the help I enjoyed while raising my children, I always made it a point to make our bed every morning. My husband queried me about this at first, and my reply was instantaneous: I wanted our children to make their own beds and if they saw me being spoiled, how could I stop them from rebelling?

Never mind that a child cannot make hospital corners too neatly; it is the effort that counts. The maid can remake it, but I feel it is important to set an example. If you want your children to grow up into spoiled brats turned adult, do not discipline them when they speak rudely to the household help. On the other hand, they can grow into nice people who know how to treat other people with respect if they learn early on how to show consideration to someone making their life abroad easier. Depending on age, some children will grow extremely attached to your helper, usually enough to drive a mother into a jealous rage from time to time. This cannot be helped, and grinning and bearing it is the only solution, unless it is a case where the child never sees his parent and is reaching out for any affection offered. Consider that before going off on a tirade. Other mothers worry about attachments that will eventually have to be broken. On that point, there are several schools of thought and you have to decide which one you will follow.

In my nuclear family, which started out as a rotational foreign service family, it would have been difficult to ask all of us not to make attachments just because they would eventually have to be broken. We have followed the philosophy that says any attachment (and this applies to friends as well as pets) is worth having, even for a short time. We could live our whole lives giving up relationships just because they were not going to be too permanent. Nothing is permanent, and there is more to be gained by having loved a little than by having loved not at all. If a nanny is good to your children, the relationship cannot hurt and will be remembered fondly in the future.

It is also worth reminding readers here that you must never forget the woman who looked after your child as a baby or toddler. Expats tend to leave a country behind without giving another thought to that caregiver who was so extremely important to your family. I was lucky enough to meet up with our Thai caregiver, Suporn, more than fifteen years after she looked after Lilly in Bangkok and was given the opportunity to show her pictures, to tell her how well Lilly had turned out due in no small part to the sense of security Suporn had given my daughter with her love and warmth. A year later, sadly, Suporn died prematurely of cancer in her mid-fifties. As I mourned the loss of this fine woman, I was nevertheless grateful that I had been given the chance to thank her.

Help And Discipline
At the same time you want your children to respect your help and not be little bullies ordering them around, you have to con-

sider how you want your help to treat your children. The discipline issue usually involves lack of, rather than too much. You may have to physically restrain a maid or amah from spoiling your kid to death.

A nanny is not a parent, and while you may want her to be as strict as possible and not let your child walk all over her, she also is not the one to hand out discipline. That is *your* job as a parent. One of the reasons I feel I was lucky on our overseas postings is that I ended up with help who were loving but firm with my children.

Quick Tips

Here is a list of useful things you need to know if you have help while living overseas. Some of it may sound like simple common sense, but you never know how easy it is to overlook such issues when you are starting out in a new country.

Tips and tipping

Be sure you know what time of year your help expects to be tipped. Chinese New Year's or year's end, national holidays, religious holidays, even a birthday could be the time of year your help, depending on the country, will receive a bonus or a cash present. Make sure you know the going rate and how many of the other helpers around you (guards and gardeners, for example) also need to be tipped. Also remember that if you stay for a few days with someone with help, it is considered gauche not to tip them for helping to make your visit pleasant (and likely doing your laundry). Be sure to ask your hostess what guidelines she may have set.

Insurance

Our Thai maid had her leg crushed under a motorcycle cab (a *tuk-tuk,* once the blight on Bangkok traffic), and although she was not working for us that day, we still felt responsible for her well-being. If she had been injured on the job, we would have been liable. Most insurance companies overseas offer something resembling a workers' compensation policy, and it is worth having just in case.

Telephone calls

One of the things that confirmed I had a gem in my Taiwanese amah was that she never once received or made a phone call while I was in the apartment. To me, that was a sign of a real professional (which she was). Since everyone carries cell phones these days, the worries about blocking your own line will be less than in my day, but someone is there to work, not to speak with their friends all day. Emergencies are one thing; idle chit-chat with the amah next door is entirely another.

Outside errands

I had a friend in Taipei who went positively nuts when she used to send her amah out for a loaf of bread and she would disappear for two hours, usually returning home without the bread. It is easier for you to do the outside work and let your maid stay put. The minute she goes out, you just know you will be needed elsewhere.

Leaving your children behind with the help

It is tempting to travel when you are posted abroad, and if we are being honest, it is nice to have a break from your children. Depending on the age of your children, though, it can be a difficult decision to leave your children behind with only the help. We were faced with this dilemma while living in Bangkok when we had an opportunity to travel to New Zealand. The solution we arrived at worked well, and we used it again in future situations. We moved then baby Lilly and Suporn into the house of our best friends. Our friends did not have to absorb the work of the baby because the maid was on hand, but we felt easier knowing that they were there for emergencies. In our foreign community of friends, we all shared kids and babysitters from time to time so parents could get a well-deserved break with peace of mind.

At the beginning of your overseas assignment, try to avoid leaving your children alone with a local caregiver. She may eventually become a treasured member of your family, but at the beginning she is just a scary stranger to your child.

Etiquette with your help

Remember that the person you hire is helping you out and enhancing your life, so try not to degenerate into a completely lazy person incapable of doing anything for yourself. They are doing enough for you, so heaping more upon them because you have forgotten how to do things for yourself is not fair.

Cross-cultural sensitivity

When your help sits down to a midday meal of what looks like glop, remember you are living in a foreign country where glop may be the national dish. Advise your children of their manners. What you eat may look like glop to them too. Also take some of their superstitions and beliefs in stride and try to learn from them. When my daughter was born in Bangkok, Suporn was firm in her belief that a stiff shot of scotch each evening would help shrink my uterus. Who was I to argue? When we travelled around the world on home leave, Suporn insisted on bringing food to the monks to bless our journey. I personally bought the rice.

Firing Your Maid

It is never easy to fire a person from your employ, but if your helper is driving you so crazy that her help is not worth the damage to your mental health, you should probably dismiss her from service. The standard rules of dismissal usually apply. That is, notice and compensation for at least two weeks' work.

The problem with firing help overseas is that for some inexplicable reason, you may end up on a treadmill of hiring and firing. Many women will confirm this: either you hire a helper right from the start who then stays with you for the duration of your assignment, or you hire and fire someone on an average of once a month. I am not suggesting you stick with someone who is truly unworkable, but often it is the case that the next one you hire will not be much better and the cycle will begin.

Heightened Expectations of the Quality of Service

Often this vicious cycle originates with your expectations of the quality of help that should be provided. If you are a fastidious housekeeper or the strictest of disciplinarians with your children, you run the risk of never being satisfied with the way your maid carries out her duties. You will complain the house is not as clean and tidy as it should be; she cannot cook to save her life; the sleeves of your blouses are not properly ironed; the flowers in the garden have grown too straggly, and so on.

Do not expect to hire some absolutely perfect helper capable of reading your mind. When you like your house cleaned a certain way, you may have to show your helper how to do it your way. She may still be operating under her previous madam's agenda and does not know that you expect her to vacuum daily or clean out the fridge once a week. In the first place she may not even understand the way you speak.

When we lived in Beijing, the standard of service was pretty low. (There were some exceptions, as we were lucky enough to have a cook who must be running his own five-star restaurant by now.) The city was also filthy from the coal-burning braziers then in use. So there was no point trying to find some super *ayi* to keep our apartment clean. And remember: if you were making a very minimum wage each day, chances are you would not be busting your butt to make sure window ledges or every picture were dusted every day.

Explaining About The Help To The Family Back Home

If you have had help during your stay abroad, get ready for the jokes: How's your slave? Must have been a tough life over there with all those servants, eh? You will take a lot of teasing when you return home, either on leave or for good, about the fact that you had help while living abroad. Your friends and family have not got the faintest clue, unless they themselves have lived overseas, about the necessity of having help just to survive in an alien environment, so save your breath.

Your family will just assume that you are being spoiled silly and if the truth be told, you are. Enjoy the experience. It is definitely one of the bonuses of life abroad.

7 Social Diversions
New Friends and Entertaining Distractions

Colonialism and imperial-style entertainments may have gone the way of the British Raj, but the rigid social "niceties" and petty social circuits that were literary fodder for the likes of Somerset Maugham and George Orwell are still, unfortunately, followed to the letter in many foreign communities. In other words, I am not entirely convinced that the dinner parties one sees in British period pieces in movies or on television, with tables set lavishly for two dozen people and butlers serving each guest, cannot be found playing out somewhere in the world today. I know, because I still see such ridiculous social tableaux being played out before my egalitarian eyes.

"And what is your husband's position in the embassy?" a newly arrived diplomatic wife may be asked while she frantically balances teacup and a slice of some freshly baked specialty of her hostess's cook.

"He's a second secretary in the foreign aid section," may be the response from a woman uninitiated into the intricate business of social stratification.

"Oh." The response is curt but always polite, cutting the new wife dead before she can even wipe the crumbs from her lips. It is delivered completely deadpan, with eyes glazed over by a total lack of social interest, while the person posing the question then moves on to the next and hopefully higher ranked new face at the coffee morning.

This is not to say that members of business communities overseas cannot be equally as guilty as diplomats in clinging to ludicrous and anachronistic pecking orders as if they were lifelines. However, based on my own bias (against), or just from my own jaded experience, where I have seen with my own eyes the scene I just described (and had it played out on me, much to my dismay), overseas bureaucrats often seem more obvious and odious in their pretentious displays of self-importance. My patience runs thin with those diplomatic wives who forget they revert back to ordinary mortals the moment their plane lands back in their own country.

Whenever I used to complain about these snobs and their social behaviour based on completely inflated convictions of position and influence, my husband would quickly remind me that diplomats achieve their sense of well-being from order, and particularly social order when abroad. Business people, as he would always point out, had routes other than social snobbery open to them for achieving personal satisfaction. They could go off and count their money. At least they used to be able to do that.

Misunderstanding the Pecking Order

When you are new to international life, you may wonder how expatriates can possibly tolerate living in foreign communities that adhere to completely intangible class structures. The unfortunate answer is that many expatriates always have and will continue to live by these arbitrary social conventions. It forms the basis of their overseas lives. Without them, they would be lost.

A true story: when my husband was a third secretary in Bangkok, we were accidentally invited to a reception hosted by the Thai prime minister in honour of the King's birthday. I say "accidentally" because the invitation was not addressed to the diplomat in the family, but to the journalist, me.

Most of the foreign press corps in Bangkok were old hands at this particular annual event and gave it a pass. Not us. We were still new to Bangkok, thought it would be a lark, and so, going against my own rule (which was to skip all diplomatic parties unless I knew the food was going to be good), I suggested we attend. My husband foolishly went along with the idea.

We decided to allow an embassy car and driver to transport us to the affair instead of chauffeuring ourselves as we normally did in our beat-up, ten-year-old Mazda (with western Canadian frost shields plastered to the windows and block heater plugs dangling out the front). This was fortunate for us, because when approaching the venue, a tremendously pillared palace with a sweeping front drive, we found ourselves in a lineup of Mercedes, carrying bored-looking bejewelled guests waiting to be discharged at the front door.

At the next queue, this one made up of people and not livery, we ran into our own Canadian ambassador and his wife, who looked surprised to see us in the reception line. In a quick exchange of pleasantries, we discovered the invitations had been issued to only the top and number two diplomats of each mission. I started to sweat in my Thai silk.

"Let's bolt," I pleaded with my husband only moments before shaking the prime minister's hand.

Negative. "Are you out of your mind?" This was followed by a stage whisper likely designed to exonerate him from responsibility for our gaffe: "You're the journalist. You're the one who suggested we come in the first place."

Luckily for us, our ambassador was wonderful and made the necessary introductions seem painless as we all carried on into the palace.

That was the last anybody spoke with us that evening. Diplomatic "niceties" were in full swing. We were nobodies, unworthy of conversation. We wandered around aimlessly until we figured out we were a lowly ranked island unto ourselves. We had to be mature about this, we assured each other. Naturally, we started to giggle and could not stop. Seizing the precise moment we could politely leave, I finally got my wish to bolt. The only balm to our egos was a glimpse of the Nepalese ambassador. In full national dress, which included a pink scarf around his head, he also wandered around in a daze. Apparently he did not know anybody either.

Socializing When You First Arrive

Even the most experienced expatriates will tell you that it is not easy to feel socially at ease when you are part of a newly arrived couple at a posting abroad. You are blank slates, individually and as a couple, and those people you come into contact with will invariably wait to see how the slate is filled in before making any moves.

Your husband's job is the first and primary criterion on which you are judged, especially the rank his job carries, whether it is diplomatic or financial, academic, or military. On first glance, you are who you are married to, and any initial social interchange will stem from his status. People will slot you—and either proceed or stop dead in their tracks—based on that most dreaded of all questions, some variation on the scenario I have described, which always comes down to this: "And what does your husband do?"

Until you get your social bearings and shake your initial feelings of culture shock, which can also bring with it complete social disorientation, not to mention insecurity, these discriminatory and subjective social judgments will seem like yet another hardship to endure, along with hot weather or language barriers. They should be treated the same, though, because eventually, not unlike the other shocks of a new culture, you will become accustomed to them and adjust your life accordingly.

By the way, not all foreign communities are necessarily rigid, but there is a hint of these misnamed social "graces" everywhere. On our posting to Taiwan, where the diplomatic community is sparse due to Taiwan's international standing, the first thing I noticed was the absence of social protocol. I immediately attributed the more relaxed atmosphere to the limited number of diplomats. When I pointed this out to various corporate wives, I was informed that social ranking did indeed exist. Among various larger multinational corporations, where the expatriate positions numbered more than half a dozen, there was in fact a pecking order, as petty as the best of them.

And there were other instances of social ranking in Taipei: in cases where an expatriate husband was heavily involved in deal making, the couple kept most of their night-time entertainment limited to people who could advance business ventures. The nurturing of new friendships was not as important a goal as the pursuit of money.

We were lucky in Taipei: as Rodney was a mere Mandarin language student at the time, we were completely off the social scale, irrelevant politically and out of touch economically. These factors had the surprising effect of liberating us totally, and we actually enjoyed a year of intense partying with people who sought us out for mere friendship, as opposed to the usual contact in what I call "counterpart" friendships. Sometimes it is more fun to be ordinary mortals overseas.

On the other hand, it is never fun to be on the receiving end of someone else's racial prejudices. Families who move from the developing countries to the Western world may at some point face the issue, even if it comes strictly in some benign form of racial ignorance. (A Taiwanese friend who moved to Canada said she was often mistaken in shopping malls as a Canadian First Nations person.) Unfortunately, there is no surefire piece of advice to offer here on how to deal with prejudice other than the general theme I have been threading throughout this book: be true to yourself and about yourself. Self-confidence goes a long way towards silencing verbal barrages of prejudice. And be sure to watch out for signs that your children are also on the receiving end of it and unable to cope. They may not have the emotional maturity to dismiss prejudice and will need your help as a mother to explain why it exists.

Insecurity in the Early Days

Why are people snobs? If taken to mean socializing only with known quantities instead of the pretentious, petty behaviour I have mentioned earlier, snobbery makes people feel safe inside a warm and secure social cocoon. A person enters a room and knows everybody there, everybody knows them, and the party begins.

As a newly arrived wife, you will feel desperately unsure of yourself and your ability to ever break into that cocoon, that is, the various social cliques. In the early days it can be tough to gain admittance and not only because of your husband's status, but because nobody knows what kind of person *you* are yet. Expatriates are often accused of engaging in instant friendships, but even by an accelerated expatriate time frame, do not expect to have instant friends within mere days of your arrival. It takes a few get-togethers to have even the slightest history of shared good times on which to form the basis of a friendship. In other words, do not instantly dismiss your powers of making new friends and get even more desperately insecure about yourself, on the basis of a twenty-minute chat over coffee that you feel led nowhere. Remember that those close friends you have back home have been friends for years, not mere minutes. And bear in mind your frame of mind: as a jet-lagged, culture shocked, stressed-out mother of young children trapped in a hotel room for eight hours without help, it is not that easy to make a good first impression.

By the way, those insecure feelings can be even further compounded if a husband and wife are not just newcomers to a certain country, but to expatriate life itself. They may find themselves standing around listening to conversations about far-flung places they can barely find on the map. Everyone, it will seem, has lived hither and yonder, or travelled there (airplane stories are very popular at expatriate functions), and the new expats will feel overwhelmed by an inability to contribute to the conversation.

Experience has to be earned, there is no way around that, but eventually you too will have stories to share. In the meantime, remember that every storyteller needs a good audience, so play that role to the hilt. And read, read, read. Be current about the affairs of your host culture. The market for travel books, in print and online, has exploded. The material is just out there, waiting for you to read. And do not worry. It does not take long to fit in. Your first home leave or trip in the region will give you a few of your own traveller's tales.

Protocol: Official and Just Plain Mean

What is a protocol? My dictionary offers a reasonable definition that can easily apply to overseas life: "a code of diplomatic or military etiquette and precedence." The reason I like my dictionary's meaning is that while it stresses etiquette (which I will address eventually, I promise), it also mentions the idea of precedence. I have lived my entire life fleeing from conformity. I suppose that makes me a protocol basher, but it is my opinion that everyone needs an escape valve when living overseas, and breaking from protocol is so far not punishable by death.

As a wife, it *is* possible to break from protocol in some instances without destroying your husband's career. Do not let him convince you otherwise. You need to be able to escape from suffocating social rules overseas, because so many of them were made over a hundred years ago and should be stuffed away in a trunk along with white gloves and hats. Life is claustrophobic enough in a small foreign community without your own culture imposing rigid rules of behaviour that have no relation to modern women.

For instance, I like to make friendships on the basis of mutual empathy and interests, not because a woman is the wife of a useful contact for my husband. When we lived abroad, I equally despised the tyrannical rules that dictated I be standing by my husband's side at every cocktail party, dinner party, or social event of the hour. If these soirées happened to fall during the dinner hour, in a city that required my spending an hour or more in bumper-to-bumper traffic, to arrive hot and sweaty for a function that might last another twenty-five minutes after I finally get there . . . well, "Forget it!" is what I used to say. I simply did not go, regardless of who the event was being held for. It was my husband's role to go to official functions. I had other things to do, like putting our children to bed.

The unwritten rule that said my presence was required was also written long before expatriate women pursued meaningful work of their own while abroad, and at a time when household help became surrogate parents. If a woman really is interested in going, that is another matter, but nobody should be forced. If a woman's absence reflects badly on her husband, we're back to the "Mad Men" mindset of the middle of the last century again.

By the same token, however, stuffy, chauvinistic protocol should not exclude women from social events if they are interested in getting out for the evening. This happens in one or two ways. There are some cultures that simply do not include women in night-time entertainment. When we lived in Korea, for example, I was not invited to dinner parties being held in my own home.

Respecting another culture—even the most extreme male chauvinism—more or less goes with the territory. It is easier to understand, though, when it is a foreign culture excluding women. But in some instances, it can be a woman's own husband who is shutting her out. Too many times, a husband will dismiss the wife from an event with the words "It's only for the office staff," then proceed to stay out long after midnight while the wife twiddles her thumbs back home wondering where he is and with whom. (I have more to say on the subject of infidelity in chapter 9.)

Expatriate wives are too often the hapless social victims of protocol, real or contrived, while their husbands in a very typical overseas situation seem to have the best of all possible worlds. The men are better equipped to deal with many of the arbitrary rules of foreign society because ultimately their work will help them to block out any ruthless inequities and get on with their lives. Protocol may be a pain for the man sometimes, but it just does not get in his way on a daily basis. He can too often use it to his advantage.

The wife, meanwhile, not only often feels left out by her own husband, but she can also be literally stuck in neutral, her wheels spinning because of protocol. This is where the petty, subjective, pretentious form of protocol usually comes in, when a woman literally has a door slammed in her face, or a friendship halted that might otherwise have blossomed. Her self-confidence may be destroyed to the point she is convinced it must be her breath or something else that has stopped people from phoning her up. By the time she realizes it is just narrow-minded social inequities or worse, a philandering husband, she may have become a complete emotional zombie. Or returned home, shattered.

One final word on snobbery for now: remember that there are snobs everywhere, even at home. In a small overseas community, though, snobbery will seem more annoying and interfering because your community has shrunk, and your self-esteem may be at an all-time low from the other adjustments you are making.

So follow the path of common sense. Get on with your life the best way you know how and make your own efforts at friendship. Learn to ignore the people who place too much emphasis on intangibles. Trust your own instincts about the people you do want to get to know better. It *is* possible to lead a satisfying life without getting all caught up in social orders, but success will definitely depend on your own attitude. And if it is the case that it is your own husband who carries rank, ignore the inevitable obsequious sycophants.

The Jerk Theory

This is a good point to introduce my own theory of social intercourse abroad because sometimes you may wrongly—and too quickly—dismiss a potential friend as a jerk, a nobody, a wimp, or any other words you may want to use to describe someone you do not intend to pay further attention to.

My theory usually plays out this way: You are at a cocktail party or dinner party and you are introduced to someone (it can be a man or a woman). The person who brought you together is called away to another conversation and you are left making small talk with this new face. The other person may be (a) sweating like crazy; (b) drunk as a skunk; (c) talking too much or too loudly; (d) constantly dropping things like a napkin or a plate of hors d'oeuvres; or (e) experiencing rapid eye movement around the room to the exclusion of your own face.

What a jerk, you think, and plot how to get away as quickly as possible. The first impression has been bad, and were you at home, you would likely avoid setting eyes on the person again. But in a small overseas foreign community, you probably will meet again. And on the second meeting, you may discover the following facts: (a) the night you met, the person was newly arrived and had brought all the wrong clothing (their light-weight clothing was still too heavy for the warm climate and they finally had just found the time to buy some lighter clothes, which put a stop to the constant sweating, which was getting downright embarrassing); (b) the last time you met, it is explained, the person had not had a chance to eat anything all day because of a bad stomach bug and had foolishly downed a drink too quickly and had got positively snapped; hence (c) he/she had found herself babbling like crazy at a drunkenly high pitch; and (d) dropping everything in sight. Finally, (e) the person who had brought him/her (not the introducer) and was supposed to take him/her home had seemingly vanished from the party and no matter where he/she frantically looked, the person was not to be found. It turns out a wild taxi cab ride back home had put the capper on that particular evening.

You find this person as entertaining as can be while confessing this litany of culture shocked woe, and you think how fortunate it was to have run into each other again because your first impression was most definitely wrong.

You have learned a valuable lesson: overseas, the benefit of the doubt should be exercised beyond the normal boundaries of home. People are uptight when they have moved to a foreign country. First impressions are very often negative because the person was uncomfortable for a variety of reasons. Remember that you probably appeared in a similar unflattering light in your first few months. Give everyone a chance. You may make a good friend that way. On the other hand, if on the subsequent two or three meetings the person does not seem to improve, really is a jerk in fact, you can keep your distance.

What to Wear: Dress Not to Be Depressed

I have always been a self-conscious person about clothes, preferring to dress for myself and saying to hell with everyone else even while fretting miserably about it. When we were posted briefly to New York City, I could barely force myself out the apartment hotel door if I did not feel I could blend in with the well-dressed and definitely well-heeled humanity on the sidewalks below. If you are a person whose indecisiveness causes her to rip apart her closet before social events, day outings, even just to hang around the house, be careful: when you are making a cultural transition to a new county, often with dramatic changes in climate, the contents of your wardrobe can have an equally dramatic effect on the state of your mind.

Not only will you be dealing with the sartorial styles and codes of the host culture, but the way in which the expatriate culture dresses may also contribute to your angst, especially at social functions. You do not necessarily want to stand out—or worse yet, be singled out for a major gaffe—but how were you to know the rest of the wives took "informal" to mean dresses and stockings when back home the same dress code meant sweat suits?

Dress up rather than down in the early days for parties. Often the venue will also help you select your clothes. Receptions held at hotels or other public places are usually fancier than at-home parties. Take note of social customs as well. For example, in Muslim countries, short, tight skirts are frowned upon, especially at official functions and other ceremonies where religion is involved.

Attending a Dinner Party Versus Cocktail Party

Most people have a preference and I advise women to pick theirs if they intend to try to limit their attendance at official entertainments. Personally, as a guest, I tend to choose the dinner party, especially the sit-down variety. My reason is simple: at a dinner party you can actually have a conversation with someone, because people cannot walk around eating a full-course meal. It is a stationary event, at least the dinner portion of it. Because I had designated my preference, I tended to go almost exclusively to dinner parties when I could not possibly get out of attending an official/diplomatic function.

Mind you, being seated (trapped by a table) does have its own drawbacks. I was once trapped between an empty chair and the guest of honour at a dinner party hosted by the apostolic pronuncio in Bangkok. On my left was a high-ranking and much-beloved Canadian cardinal, known for his amazing endeavours in support of the poor in Africa and Asia. He was not my problem. On the contrary, we had spent an enjoyable afternoon at a Thai orphanage, where I had the privilege of interviewing this eighty-year-old priest after he had enchanted the orphans by riding on an elephant. I was delighted to have the opportunity to speak to him some more. But seated on *his* left was an elderly Canadian nun, a long-standing resident of Thailand, who was not about to be upstaged by this babbling Jewish woman who in her view had been mistakenly seated next to this important Catholic personage. I could hear her mind ticking over: What was the pronuncio thinking by seating her there?

As for cocktail receptions, the reason I chose to avoid going to them was because I felt they tended to be flighty affairs and still do to this day. People perch on each other, like birds, for mere seconds before spotting another prey and flying off. The conversations, which only last mere seconds, are typically pointless and often surreal. In my view, cocktail parties are too short given the time commitment. You always end up all dressed up with nowhere to go.

Hosting Parties

As a diplomatic hostess, my preference was reversed: I preferred giving a cocktail reception any day over a sit-down dinner for twelve, unless it was for twelve close friends. As a hostess, with a thousand and one things on your mind, the distraction factor can be too high to be able to concentrate on any worthwhile conversation. Therefore, a cocktail party was ideal, especially overseas where language barriers came into play as well as the regular cocktail party challenges.

I liked being able to constantly excuse myself and head off to confer with the hired help (who were actually doing all the work for the evening). At your own dinner party, you have to be polite and smile a lot at some visiting widget salesman or politician. The latter tended to be easier because they see everyone as a potential voter and treat everyone with equal friendliness.

Before we leave the subject of parties altogether, though, here are a few of my own serious, and a few irreverent, tips on etiquette for giving and surviving them:

- Be aware of the cultural or religious persuasions of your guests, especially if you are living in a Muslim country where alcohol and pork are taboo; for Hindus, beef is forbidden.
- If you have to give a lot of dinner parties, experienced hostesses recommend you keep a record of what food and wine you served to whom on what date so you do not repeat yourself (some women like to keep track of what they wore as well).

- Make sure you have enough help if it is your party. In most foreign communities, there are freelance waiters who work nights helping the expatriates entertain each other.
- Women with tendencies towards heated debate should make every effort to restrict themselves to bland conversation and small talk at expatriate social functions that are devoid of any substance for the women participants: learn to speak only about what you have recently purchased at some ridiculously small sum.
- Eat before you go to either dinner or a cocktail party, for overseas the former tends to begin late and the latter offers few distractions other than hors d'oeuvres. This technique also helps stop you from stationing yourself in front of the food table.
- As a hostess, never invite anyone far above your own social ranking, for this can lead to a very dull and quiet party if the guests feel there is no one there they can speak to, especially the host and hostess.
- Decide if you plan to be an air kisser or not. I find it ridiculous to kiss people I have met only once or twice, but air kissing is rampant on the expatriate circuit, and a consistent position should be adopted before heading out into the social whirl. At the same time, remember the social etiquette of other countries, which may, for instance, forbid any physical contact (including shaking hands) between members of the opposite sex unless they are blood relations.

Other Distractions

Life overseas is not just one long cocktail party. There are other frivolous amusements that can distract the expatriate wife who chooses not to seek employment, study the language, or take any highbrow cultural courses. I would like to say at the outset that while this discussion will likely be viewed as tongue in cheek, and in part it is meant to make fun of myself and others like me, I have engaged in every last one of these diversions at one time or another.

Going to the hairdresser

The BBC, known for its bizarre documentaries on everything from rare wildlife to outer space, once explored in detail the life of another offbeat species, namely the expatriate wife. In this particular documentary, the wives in question lived in Hong Kong. I am singling out this program because during the interviews, one of the Hong Kong expatriate wives made a comment that is relevant to this discussion of life overseas. She said, "There is no excuse for a woman not to be well-groomed in Hong Kong." I laughed so hard I thought my husband's British cousins, with whom I was watching the program, were going to think there was something wrong with me. I could not possibly explain to them well enough that the comment was simply perfect.

Going to the hairdresser is one of the most common distractions for expatriate wives. I happen to enjoy washing my own short curly hair in the shower and rarely have time for anything but a botched home manicure, but there is absolutely no need for one to engage in this manual labour on some postings, and many women do not. Perfect hair, nails, and toes can be seen as part of the uniform of an expatriate wife. Hanging out in beauty parlours can take up a good part of the morning and certainly kill the time before meeting someone for lunch.

Tennis

This is another popular pastime of the expatriate wife, along with golf where available. Most expatriate clubs in foreign settings will offer various leagues and tournaments, which can essentially allow women to play every day if they wish. If you decide to play in any expatriate wives' league, make sure you are good at the sport. There are some women who have channelled so much of their frustrated creative energy into tennis that a simple match can become a very serious proposition.

Shopping

I have told people over the years that I failed miserably as an expat wife because I hate to shop. But there can be no end to shopping bonanzas for the overseas wife, for in addition to shops with easy local access, most international women's clubs arrange for a variety of day excursions to other shopping opportunities that may not be easy to reach on your own. I do not have any personal experience with these excursions. (My own shopping style is limited to complete blow-outs in bookstores around the world, although I have been known to have a complete personality change when presented with the consumer smorgasbord in Hong Kong.) However, I have been told that bargains and exotica abound on these day trips. Shopping tours are also arranged within various regions. This is certainly the case within the Asian sphere, where expatriate wives fly off in groups of half a dozen or more to major shopping capitals in Korea, Hong Kong, Singapore, and Thailand. I am told that these junkets provide a perfect outlet for women who like to "shop till they drop" because cultural sights are normally not included on these tours in order to maximize spending time.

Bitch and stitch luncheon groups

There are variations of this theme everywhere but its essence should be obvious. Women gather to complain about maids, husbands, and overseas life generally while sewing, viewing a fashion show, learning how to arrange flowers, and other wifely activities.

Having a baby

This option is limited to certain age groups, but from personal experience this is a wonderful way to distract you during your overseas posting. There are medical appointments, prenatal classes, city-wide searches for baby things, and lots of guilt-free napping and eating associated with this activity. After the birth, there are exercise classes and playgroups to fill your day.

Entertaining visitors from home

This activity is usually accompanied by high levels of stress, depending on where you are posted in the world. If you have adequate help and the city is not completely chaotic, you will have an easier time of it because your guests will be inclined to venture out by themselves. Otherwise, you can end up with guests who prefer never to leave your home, even after it has been pointed out to them that they have travelled thousands of miles to virtually be prisoners in an apartment or house.

Part of the problem of entertaining friends and family from home is that, depending on the distance they have travelled, they feel obliged to stay for at least a month. Try to limit your hospitality to two weeks maximum or silent screaming will become your new pastime. Also attempt to set ground rules before arrival such as: guests are required to spend a certain number of hours on their own each day in order for the hostess to recover her cool. If it is a mother-in-law coming to visit, absolutely insist that your husband take time off before letting her in the door. Plan these visits well ahead of time, and where possible, do advance work on all excursion destinations. Try to avoid arriving anywhere sight unseen, especially with parents.

Making Friends

I will try to be more serious now, because making friends overseas is serious business. Ask a woman how she survived a difficult posting (ask me about Taiwan, for instance) and she will more often than not tell you it was because of some wonderful friend who pulled her through. Sure, activities and projects and clubs all provide distractions, but everyone needs at least one soul mate, someone with whom they share complete empathy.

In a foreign environment, where many things are unfamiliar, a best friend can be like a security blanket to be dragged around with you. If you are not together, you are checking in with one another to compare that day's horror stories or achievements. Your friend is your point of contact with a new order of living.

Many of these friendships will seem to happen by sheer serendipity, but mutual interests or stage of life is usually a powerful incentive. Although some initial factor may spark acquaintance, many shared interests are usually learned in those incredible first conversations of discovery.

I had only been living in Bangkok long enough to confirm I was pregnant with my first child when I started a Thai language class for expatriate wives. Sitting in a row along an open window (the school had an open-air concept, allowing the clatter of geese and chickens from a courtyard below to effectively shut out the teachers' voices), about eight of us dependents sat fanning ourselves, myself especially since the early days of pregnancy were not my most comfortable. We were learning the Thai word for our various nationalities. When a woman down the row said she was from Canada, followed by my own declaration only moments later, we both quietly leaned forward to get a better look at our fellow countrywoman. Later, after class, we naturally sought each other out, only to discover we were about two weeks apart in our pregnant condition both for the first time, and the friendship blossomed from there. I simply could not have survived without her (we are best friends to this day) and other soul mates I was lucky enough to connect with in Taipei, Beijing, and Seoul.

There are lots of ways besides women's meetings to make new friends. One absolutely foolproof way is through the international schools, but this naturally will only hold true for women travelling with children. Parent organizations have highly trained radar for seeking out volunteers for absolutely everything, and someone will likely contact you before your last box is unpacked. You do not need to go the official route either to make friends through the school. Simply ask your son or daughter who they may wish to play with after school, and presto, you are on the phone to another woman.

Language classes, mothers' groups, health clubs, or super-market checkouts can all be scouted for new friends, if you are proactive in reaching out. You will not necessarily like everyone you meet, but foreign communities offer few shortages of people to try out, bearing in mind all the social "niceties" I mentioned earlier. Where there are no built-in communities offered by corporate families or embassies, remember that you will have to muster up your own self-confidence to phone up people and arrange meetings. No one can do this for you.

Your local neighbours as well as the wives of your husband's local colleagues are valuable friends to have. You can meet local people in other situations too, such as at work, at prenatal classes, in church, in local choirs, at health clubs, or in public libraries. The possibilities are endless. What is important is the willingness to overcome that "local/expatriate" barrier, which unfortunately often includes a subconscious racial barrier. Sad but true. Initially, exchanges are brief and sometimes awkward, but eventually there will come a moment when you can suggest a cup of coffee together or lunch and a wonderful friendship blossoms.

Shaking Friends

We are all eager to please when we first move somewhere new, and in our eagerness and naïveté we sometimes tend to reach out and touch virtually everyone. Unfortunately, we sometimes embrace friendships that we quickly discover are not meant to be. The dilemma then arises: how to escape a bad situation in a small community. The chance of not bumping into a person again is pretty slim.

Friendships that stop cold because of lack of common ground as opposed to lack of social standing or due to a major disagreement are bound to happen overseas just as they might happen at home. You may begin a friendship with the best of intentions, but conversation quickly fades to nothing, or you discover you simply cannot stand the way her kids treat yours. There are a thousand and one reasons.

Be polite about it if you run into one of those never-to-be-friends. If you feel like it was going nowhere, there is a good chance she may have been thinking the same thing about you and was equally worried about how to extricate herself from an uncomfortable situation. Not every friendship that starts out easily will necessarily blossom. So when you see each other, make appropriate small talk but do not lie to each other about plans that will never be carried out. See this as a golden opportunity to get off the phony "Let's have lunch" treadmill.

Friendships that wither after a major argument or falling-out can be more problematic in small communities. Try hard not to bring other people into your fight. This makes everyone uncomfortable. If you must make more of an effort to meet people overseas, by the same token you have to be more willing to rise above petty squabbles. Agree to disagree and get on with your lives. A posting is too short to carry grudges.

Losing Friends

You will say goodbye a lot during an expatriate life. People are constantly moving on, including yourself, and sometimes it seems like you were just getting to know someone when confirmation for their next posting comes through. There is no way around this fact of life, but there are a few ways some women try to protect their emotions, not all of which I necessarily agree with.

Many women I know, especially ones who are permanent expatriates who stay in places longer than rotational people, prefer to make friends only with others whom they know will be around for a while. This certainly helps you avoid being attached to someone whose local shelf life is limited, but at the same time, you never know what a brief friendship may hold.

Recognize that you will have to say goodbye eventually and then enjoy the days together with someone whose company and opinions you value. Those capricious social codes are often unavoidable, but choosing new friends on the basis of time constraints is your own doing and can be avoided. It seems to be harder when your friends leave the post rather than vice versa, because when you are on the move, the distractions are enormous and it is hard to focus on anything but what is at hand. When a friend pulls up and leaves a hole in your daily routine, however, you will feel at a loss and slightly disoriented to be sure.

We returned to Taipei from a European holiday just after my closest friend, a Taiwanese/Canadian woman, had moved to the United States. For the first few days we were back, I thought it was jet lag that was making me feel so fuzzy and unfocused. And then it hit me: my friend was gone and I had to readjust my time accordingly. As I wrote in a letter to her shortly after she left, suddenly I could work, on this book as it happens, without distractions and it was killing me. I missed her a lot.

It sounds trite when put into words, but even though you are saying goodbye to close friends, you probably will see them again if you make the effort to keep in touch, which nowadays is easier than ever before. Organize reunions wherever possible. Any friendship, even a brief one or carried out across twelve time zones, is worth having and remembering. Such global friendships are a benefit of life abroad that cannot ever be written into a contract.

8 Home Leave to Hell
It May Not Be Heaven

I did some creative editing of *Webster's* words (I know a thing or two about taking words out of context, as I used to be a television reporter) and came up with an intriguing definition for home leave that is not too far from the reality. Home leave, given selective meanings, can be when the social unit formed by persons living together in exile, having received authorized permission to be absent from duty, departs for a congenial environment in its place of origin.

But let us forget about the dictionary, particularly that part about "a congenial environment in its place of origin." If that is supposed to mean the home of a loving family member, happy to see you all after a year, with doors thrown open to you and no emotional strings attached, then the tooth fairy *does* exist.

Yes, you can go home again, and even have a good time. But this does not happen by divine right. It requires proper planning and the adopting of realistic expectations.

What Makes Home Leave Such a Touchy Subject?
This is not a riddle. What do you call two people who cannot stop talking, fighting, eating, packing, flying, driving, packing, eating, drinking, fighting, shopping, spending, drinking, eating, etc., etc.? Answer: an expatriate couple who have just spent a fortune to be pampered and/or tortured by family on an annual home leave.

And so it follows, what do you call a person doing all of the items listed above, by herself, with several children in tow, surrounded by in-laws who drive her crazy, and immediate family who may not offer an ounce of sympathy or help because they are too resentful and/or just plain uninterested in her overseas life? Answer: an expatriate wife on home leave alone, of course!

Old hands at the game know there are three subjects over which expatriate couples can be relied upon to engage in heated argument. The first two, sex and money, do not count since you do not need to live overseas to fight about those time-honoured themes of marital discord. Home leave, on the other hand, is never a subject that can just lie there. It can be fraught with danger, debate, exhaustion, and emotional disaster.

Where to Stay

Depending on your leave entitlement and company or government benefits, the subject of home leave will normally come up about halfway through the first year abroad. It is often triggered by thoughts about family, or your old neighbourhood, or something that sets off a bout of homesickness.

It may also come up after a conversation with another wife who has informed you that the foreign community completely bolts once the international school closes for the summer. You discover that there will be nobody for you or your children to do things with, and seasonal temperatures will be high enough to induce comas. The danger begins when you begin to consider where you will stay during your home leave.

"We have to go home this summer," you will tell your husband, idealizing family members who actually annoy you and rhapsodizing over shops or streets that normally you ignore. "OK," he'll say, "but I don't want to stay with your parents for longer than a week, so we'll take a holiday somewhere before visiting my parents on the way back."

"A week?!" you'll cry. "That's not enough time! They still haven't forgiven me for taking the grandchildren out of the country. Are you crazy? I can't go home for just a week! We'll have to stay for at least two weeks, minimum."

Flash forward.

"Why did you listen to me?" you cry to your husband in the privacy of the "spare" bedroom being used as your home leave command post.

The excess baggage is piled high to the ceiling; laundry (which you may not have done personally in at least a year) litters the floor; five bags of new unopened tubes of the only toothpaste your children will brush with and twenty-four 100 percent cotton panties have been thrown carelessly on the bed after that day's five-minute reprieve, alone, in the local mall.

You turn to your husband and unburden all of it: "My mother is driving me crazy, nobody will let me sleep off my jet lag, and I'm already eating too much!!"

You have been home three days.

Second scenario: Your brother or sister fervently insisted on the availability of space in their new house, which could cozily accommodate all of you, even with their own children and pets and possibly other sleeping-over friends or relatives. It is summer-time, they laugh, when the living is easy. Throw another steak on the barbie.

That is a common idealized fantasy of a sibling relationship that may be playing on some parallel dimensional planet, but not here on earth. Think about it: if you fought like cats and dogs when you were younger and there were no wives, husbands, children, or in-laws, how can you possibly believe you will not get on each other's nerves when you and your family arrive jet-lagged and culture shocked, dragging enough luggage for an army?

Who Should You Visit?

Here is another threatening area: trying to figure out in advance which people you will allot precious, limited time to see. It is a maxim of the unwritten rules governing home leave: every known relative, and ones so distant you only remember hearing their name once, possibly mentioned by your aging grandmother, will want a piece of you when you arrive home from overseas.

So will all of your friends.

But here is the catch. Everyone wants to see you, but nobody wants to hear you. Let me set the scene once again. You walk through the door and embrace your sister or oldest girlfriend or maybe even your mother.

"It's so good to see you!!" you overlap each other, not unlike the preceding year of long-distance telephone calls down that time-delayed international voice wind tunnel. "Tell me everything!!!" your mother or sister or girlfriend manages to edge out over you.

"Well . . . ," you begin breathlessly. "We're living on the most amazing street, filled with these people who . . . " "Do you like my hair?" they interrupt within ten seconds. "There's a new hair stylist at your old beauty salon and you wouldn't believe what a mess they made of so-and-so's hair . . . "

"Is that right?" you reply, your mind—and mouth—braking to a halt. Then, quickly getting a handle on the situation, you ask, "How is so-and-so?"

"Well . . . ," they begin breathlessly. And you eat the cake/sandwich/bun/caloric what's-it already placed before you.

Another twisted Murphy's Law of home leave: you never get to spend more than thirty seconds with the friends you really want to see. Fortunately, they will understand the most and continue to stay connected when you return abroad.

And then there is the relative or friend of a friend you have to visit and who knows the country you are living in better than you do, despite the fact that they have never been there.

"I was reading an article about that place you're posted to the other day," some know-it-all will pontificate.

Depending on the state of your jet lag or the stage of your leave (tolerance levels run higher at the beginning due to excitement) you will either respond politely or ram the piece of cake you are once again eating down somebody's throat.

You smile a lot on your round of home leave courtesy calls. You develop set pieces as well. On automatic talking pilot, you will be able to give an abridged version or the documentary-length disclosure on your life overseas without actually thinking. Old hands can plan the next visit on their agenda while they seemingly gush about the new culture they are learning about.

Nobody wants to hear anything negative. After all, they figure you have an army of servants peeling you grapes all day. Dare to mention the air virus your son picked up because the local children use the street as a toilet and the comment back to you will be: "So why don't you come home?"

"Maybe because my husband's job is over there and I want my marriage to continue," you mutter, very quietly. Smile and eat your cake.

The High Price of Torture

There are three price tags attached to home leave. First there is the cost in cold hard cash. This tab can run exceedingly high depending on where you are posted. In real dollars, you may actually spend very little on airplane tickets and hotel reservations along the way, because for some expatriates, they are the typical perquisites of overseas life. Costs run high when you run head-on into conspicuous consumer consumption. Heads will turn as you buy two dozen of everything you need, maybe will need, or do not need at all but you have not seen any of whatever it is for a year.

Before our first home leave from our posting to Bangkok, Rodney and I jointly decided that we really did not need anything and would devote any spare cash to what we really needed: a good time. This, to us, meant movies, restaurants, and live entertainment. Given the size of my family (it is true, his family is small; it was *my* fault we had no time to ourselves), we were able to get to maybe one movie during a three-week leave in Toronto.

But then we decided to visit one of Toronto's biggest shopping centres, which had three levels of what amounted to everything we both absolutely had to have. Did someone drug us? Why did we suddenly pull out our charge cards and start hyperventilating in shoe stores? The sheer volume of available goods simply overwhelmed us. I have known people on home leave who have damn near fainted from joy in a Walmart. The thought of everything they needed under one roof was simply too much to handle at one time.

Also at work is what can be called "belligerent" spending habits, the kind of mass buying hysteria in stores prompted by an inner voice that says to you: "I'm enduring enough hardships living overseas. I want this. I'm going to buy it. I deserve it." Belligerent spending is curtailed only by your credit card spending limit. Ask any expatriate home leaver about the cost of their trip, and they will tell you they are still paying off their charge cards six months later because it made sense to buy a crate of everything.

And that is just the unnecessary spending. If you are posted to a country where food is limited, you truly are forced to blow your grocery budget a year in advance. The problem is, your husband's paycheque still only comes once or twice a month. There is a lot of sighing over the unavoidable hidden costs of home leave, such as rented cars and eating out in restaurants.

The other two price tags on home leave, the emotional and physical costs, are not as easy to add up. Unlike credit card receipts, you cannot just safely stash them away and total up the damage later. These costs nibble away at you every hour you are home, overlapping and fuelling each other.

The physical exhaustion of flying thousands of miles across ten or twelve time zones often makes emotional crises even harder to handle. You burst into tears because some family member is not being sensitive enough to your new life, but it could be that your crying is just from being jet-lagged and/or from sheer fatigue.

Or you feel alienated from friends and family, people who mean a lot to you, and blame it on them instead of recognizing that even on returning home for a short period of time, you may be experiencing a bit of reverse culture shock (a subject I address in chapter 10). Your own culture seems strange for a while because you have finally just gotten used to the other one over there and now this one seems alien.

Confused? Of course you are. You can get caught in a bit of a culture warp and momentarily lose your balance. You feel as if your brain has been drained of its life-sustaining fluids. You feel horribly distracted. You cannot seem to concentrate or focus your thoughts. It is easy to throw blame onto your family because, why not? We blame family for everything! In this instance, give them a break. Relax and watch television and ease back into it.

The Neutral Zone

Where to stay depends a lot on how long you choose to stay. Will it be just a few days? A week? Longer than two weeks? For just a couple of days, it *may* be all right for your emotional health to stay with family, depending on the size of their house or apartment and your relationship with them. If tension already exists for whatever reason (they hate your husband, they hate your in-laws, they are not keen on you), better take a pass on the old family dwelling.

If you plan to stay in one metropolitan area and branch out, the smartest thing you can do is to take over some vacationing person's house or rent a summer cottage. Apartment hotel suites, which are cheaper than regular hotel rooms, offer weekly rates and a kitchen.

The point is to have your own space instead of being at the mercy of anybody else. *You* are the one travelling thousands of miles and living out of suitcases. Having neutral territory means you can invite, without guilt, all the people you want to see to your place, all at once or separately. A good way to see people you do not necessarily need to visit privately is to invite them *en masse*. If it is your own place and you are doing all the work, then you are not guilt-ridden about heaping burden upon your hosts. If you are travelling with children, staying put in one place is also better for their mental health and routines, instead of bed hopping across the county or a city. Consider your disorientation, and then think how a three-year-old feels if he wakes up in the middle of the night in the fourth bed he has slept in that week.

Be ready for the tidal waves of guilt that will come crashing down around you from disappointed friends or relatives who are absolutely inconsolable that you have chosen to stay in some strange hotel or cottage. But measure that guilt against your angst when by day three, you are ready to slit your wrists and move out. In my opinion, some parents are secretly relieved when visiting expatriate children stay in neutral territory.

Before I forget to mention it, be sure to rent a car. Do not rely on friends and family to chauffeur you around. A car can mean freedom for everyone.

What to Do?

The short answer is, try not to do everything. The goal of home leave is to lead a reasonably normal life in your old culture, to become reacquainted with friends and family, and to remind yourself of where you come from and your own culture's values and way of life. You cannot do this if you schedule too many visits and appointments or embark on an endless round of dinner parties during the three weeks or so that you are home. Learn to say no. I know this is hard for some people, including myself, but declining invitations that are not absolutely necessary means you have the time to relax.

Be sure to schedule time for yourself. Take time to browse quietly in a shopping centre instead of being in a constant state of hyperactivity. It will do a lot for your mental health. You may also avoid buying frenzies if you are not rushing around like a maniac. I used to sit in my old public library and read back issues of newspapers and magazines and feel wonderful. Going to an afternoon movie and indulging in a giant bag of popcorn and super-sized Diet Coke was absolute bliss.

There will be practical issues to be addressed so do not forget to make appointments with dentists and doctors. It is often best to have some family member line those up before you even come home, since many doctors are booked months in advance. Make sure you check in with any professional looking after financial affairs for you or your lawyer. Face-to-face meetings with the people in charge of your life's affairs should also be done while you are home.

Use the phone as much as possible, especially if you are unable to visit someone living too far from where you are. Visiting people is important, but visiting *places* can be equally significant during home leave. Walk down your favourite street and remember the sounds and smells of home. Hang around a main street and listen to the conversations. Take time to read the newspapers and local magazines to catch up on your own country. If you are travelling with children, make sure you do something special for them. Children will not tolerate endless visits to nameless relatives. I have heard of some permanent expatriate American families who make a point of doing some historical sightseeing on every home visit to ensure their children get to know the America they have never lived in.

Who to Visit?

I should really turn this question around. Who should you invite to visit you? For the key to a successful home leave visit is to make sure that you are not the one trundling miles out of your way and exhausting yourself to visit someone who could more easily have visited you.

Always accommodate yourself first. That could mean scheduling the visiting hours. You are the one spaced out and distracted and exhausted and trying to fit too much into too short a period of time, with lead weights (if you have young children) attached at your ankles. If a friend or family member is unwilling to appreciate the distance you have travelled and all of the mitigating emotional factors, then they are not worth seeing anyway.

Balance each obligatory visit with something fun. Combine visits with entertainment or other points on your home leave wish list. Meet friends and go to a movie or a club or whatever you wanted to squeeze in. Meet at a museum coffee shop or art gallery. Try not to meet at too many restaurants or you will need to buy new clothes before you return abroad.

The Home Leave Diet

Laugh if you will. This may be the most important piece of advice yet. Just as you cannot do everything, it is also impossible to eat everything. You will be tempted. On my first home leave, I simply could not pass a delicatessen without stopping. It became an obsession. On a home leave from Beijing, Caesar salads became the object of my desired eating. Learn to say no to a piece of cake or buy a wardrobe the next size up. If it is not at all possible, make every attempt to lose five pounds *before* you go home. This serves the dual purpose of giving you the flexibility to ease your way back up the scale. Despite the stress of arranging home leave and fighting with your spouse, try fasting for a week before leaving.

Try to avoid airplane food. It is not critical to your health to eat four meals in ten hours, so try to eat only one meal and avoid the empty calories of alcohol. If you are travelling with your children, resist the urge to polish off their trays as well as your own.

Feeling fat is never pleasant, but you can still eat wisely and at the same time enjoy all the food you have missed for the time you have been away. Eat in moderation and do not overindulge. Be true to yourself and go ahead, face that mirror, keeping your self-image and self-worth firmly in your mind.

Naturally you cannot get regular exercise on a home leave, but you would be amazed to know how much energy you expend packing and unpacking, dragging luggage through airports where trolleys are non-existent, helping your hostess vacuum and keep her house clean out of guilt, doing laundry for the first time in a year, walking back and forth through shopping centres dazed at the plethora of goods, and so on. Many calories are also burnt off in hysteria and family burnout.

So relax about eating. You are not gaining as much weight as you might think, despite all that cake. And remember: you can also lose it anyways when you return to your post.

The Errant Husband

Worse than doing a home leave on your own is doing it with a husband who takes a powder the minute you hit his mother's house. Look out for one particular warning sign: he brings his golf clubs along.

I have heard too many tales of woe from expatriate wives who have gone this distance, only to find there are more hurdles to overcome once the journey is half done. Understandably, many men have to check in with headquarters and often get roped into "temporary duty." This cannot be helped and should be expected.

Like your life overseas, however, a battle can easily brew over whose leisure time matters more, and what exactly constitutes "leisure." If you find you are back to those "work-related" rounds of golf, let the shouting matches begin.

Make sure both of you know the parameters of each other's free time. You are entitled to time alone as much as he is, and shopping for household goods and children's clothing should not count as your leisure time. Going to lunch, for a walk, to a movie—that is "alone" time. Make sure you get some and he does not hog it all. Remind him of his share of house-hold/childcare duties.

Take Your Nanny With You

Opinion is divided on the issue of taking your nanny on home leave. Certainly if you think you have a potentially delinquent husband, it is worth some consideration. Financial restraints may throw the entire question out before it requires any thought at all. But if it is feasible, here are a few pros and cons.

Pros: If you are travelling with small children, having a built-in babysitter cannot be beat. It means you can see everyone and not be at the mercy of asking relatives to, heaven forbid, do you a favour and mind your child for the evening. It also takes a lot of stress out of long-distance flying when there is someone else to amuse the kids for twelve hours. You also get over jet lag faster because a maid/amah/ayah/nanny/ whomever lets you catch up on your sleep. When your husband stays behind and you go it alone, a helper could save your life.

Cons: Arriving home with a "servant" will spark endless conversation from family. Never mind that the people doing the teasing have had live-in help since the moment their own children were born. The fact that you have arrived with this foreign woman means you have become a *memsahib*. You can easily tell these critics to stick it you know where.

More of a problem is the maid herself. You have plucked her out of her own country and you want to be sensitive to her culture shock. You become her lifeline, and that is suffocating in the already choking environment of demanding family. Her health, what she will eat, even the clothes she may need for the new climate: all of these are considerations you must not overlook. The best advice is to rely on your own instincts that you know your maid best and should be able to gauge how she might fare as a traveller.

I am able to share my own positive experience in this area because we took Suporn from Thailand around the world with us when my daughter was just one year old. I never worried about taking her on a long trip for one instant. She handled the entire experience beautifully, allowed us the clear time to purchase our first home in a matter of days, and gave us the freedom to have a quick holiday in San Francisco at the end of our home leave, by staying put with our daughter in the hotel while we raced from movie to movie to cram it all in.

Post-Home Leave Blues

You think you're depressed about your weight? Your family? Your marriage? The fact that you think your own country is going to the dogs? Wait until you get back to your posting and experience post–home leave blues. This can often be as bad as post-partum depression if not worse. But you do get over it!

Depression upon return is not always immediately felt. First of all, you are so happy to be back in your own space, with privacy again, that often the relief you feel is almost intoxicating. This feeling lasts for about forty-eight hours. And then it hits you.

We're really back. To stay. For long-term expatriates, unlike rotational people who leave a place every two or three years, this depression can be particularly bad. Expect to feel it, because not unlike any emotionally intensive experience, you will feel let down when you come home. If you have been back on home leave to a developed country, a return to a less-developed country will be harder. Things will look less organized by comparison. Work hard at reminding yourself of the pleasures of overseas life. If that does not work, think about living full-time near your family.

Most of all get active again. Do not hang around wishing you were home. Jump back into everything as soon as possible. The feeling will pass, usually at the same time as your jet lag.

Optional Home Leave

Is it written down in your contract that you have to actually go home on your leave? If it is not, and the air tickets and hotel reservations can be used elsewhere, why not alternate home leave with interesting holiday destinations instead? When we were living in Bangkok and needed a Western environment for a break, we chose to go to Australia and New Zealand instead of going home to Canada. Admittedly, we did not see family on that holiday, but we did soak up that Western ambience we were missing without the emotional hassles.

Or instead of going home and returning straight back to your post, schedule a holiday somewhere new on the return portion. Incidentally, this option works best if you want to get home right away. Coming back, you often need to stop and decompressurize your brain.

We stopped for five days in San Francisco after our first home leave and managed to do everything we were not able to do in Canada—watch television, go to movies and restaurants, even read for longer than twenty minutes without somebody offering us a piece of cake. It was worth the extra expense. Likewise, returning to Beijing after a month in Canada, we rested our mouths (from talking; we still ate like crazy) in Vancouver. It was a nice transitional phase and allowed us to get some last-minute relaxation time.

If It's So Bad, Why Do We Do It?

I hate to get sentimental about this, it may be positively jarring after my cynicism, but whenever I have asked people in the throes of a torturous home leave why on earth they are doing it, the shrug of their shoulders suggests the same answer an exhausted new parent would give to someone asking them why they had children.

We go home for some of the same reasons we choose to marry and have children. It is part of the life cycle that somehow cannot be denied. In the expatriate life cycle, the urge to return home and touch base with the people we love and the culture that has shaped our lives just cannot be helped.

You know it will not be easy; but it pays to also know what to expect, and what *not* to expect, from the people and places you are going to see. So go with your eyes open and hope for the very best.

9 Guilt and Resentment
The Expatriate Couple's Extra Baggage

"In a marriage overseas, what else *is* there besides guilt and resentment?"

I was supposed to be the person asking the questions, but that one was posed to me by an American expatriate wife living at the time in Taipei. To an outsider, she would seem the type of woman who had successfully adapted to overseas life. Extremely outgoing and talented, she appeared to be living a full professional life abroad while simultaneously raising three children under the age of nine. At the time I spoke to her, she was working full-time at a variety of writing and communications jobs in addition to being a major volunteer force in the local foreign community. In the few fleeting uncommitted moments she had in her overloaded day, she confessed her fantasy was a simple one: she dreamed of having time for herself.

Her question to me had been purely rhetorical, but it was not much different from a number of similarly cynical and resigned responses I received when surveying other women for comments on how they handled burning resentment and guilt, the components of the emotional time bomb that ticks away for the duration of many couples' overseas assignments. These feelings are especially intense when a husband has brought his wife and family thousands of miles to an unfamiliar land and then flees from all responsibilities, except his career. The 24/7 on-demand world of the twenty-first century has meant most working husbands are focused on work over family.

My Taipei friend used many words to describe a not uncommon expatriate phenomenon in which women cope with an internal battle between their negative emotions, including bitterness, estrangement, shame, remorse, and alienation, and the positive feelings of love and support they show for their spouses.

In the final analysis, though, many of the conversations I initiated on the subject came down to two words: *his fault*.

"Overseas," my friend said, "men simply resign from family life. I never expected that my own husband wouldn't be there to help raise his family. He is never home before eight at night and often has work to do on weekends. He's too tired for us to entertain friends but there's always time for business."

"So is there hope?" I asked my Taipei friend.

"I don't know that we'll ever work it out. He feels guilty and I feel furious." And then she laughed.

"This hell is here to stay," she joked. "So I better have a sense of humour about it."

'What Fresh Hell Is This?'

Dorothy Parker, the witty American writer and former expatriate herself, albeit in the glorious days of France in the 1920s, was reported to have always posed this query in response to a ringing telephone. Many decades later, her famous *bon mots* could easily be adapted for the modern-day expatriate wife. What fresh hell and potential emotional danger lies in store when her husband signals the start of his conversation with the words "Dear, you may not like this, but I have to (blank) . . . " Fill in with one or more of the following:

- Go out of town for a two-week business trip right after arrival.
- Work late tonight at the office/embassy/base.
- Take a client out for dinner and you're not invited and take still another client golfing both Saturday and Sunday.
- Drag you to a cocktail party I know you do not want to go to/ask you to give a dinner party you do not want to give.

- Miss taking the kids to their doctor's appointments even though I promised I would because I have to work on an important presentation.
- Inform you that you will not be able to work at that job you wanted so much because the host government/the embassy/the company/I will not allow it.
- Take the car for the next few weeks while some client is in town.
- Cancel the holiday we planned for just the two of us, because some important honcho from headquarters is arriving.
- Send you off to do home leave by yourself with the kids because I cannot get away.
- Move us to some other godforsaken place because that job will be even more wonderful for my career and/or worth a lot of money to us.

Overseas, these and other similar scenarios can always be counted on to provide a surefire spark for igniting major confrontations, involving heavy salvos of guilt and resentment. The wife will seldom emerge victorious from such showdowns—or happy.

Let us examine each one separately. Then you will have no excuse for saying you did not know what you were getting into. But first let me provide one caveat to this discussion: I will be describing the worst-case scenario. Nobody could be as bad as some of the husbands who will crop up in the following pages, although I have personally run into many who come perilously close. Still, I plan to offer a few consoling words in the husband's defense, including one point that should be stated at the outset: many men behave abominably because their wives allow them to. Some women do not raise a fuss until it is too late. Remember this too: your husband is not a mind reader. You must tell him what you need.

On the Road Again

You have barely unpacked the boxes when your husband returns home from his new office and announces he has to go away for a few days or even a few weeks. He makes it clear he has no choice in the matter, and furthermore, he warned you there would be travel involved in this new job so do not look so surprised.

Sure, you heard about this before you left, but back home you still had all that excitement pumping through you, and your friends and family were nearby. Now that you have arrived in a foreign city, the news stuns you because you just did not expect the issue would arise so quickly. You are barely over your jet lag. School will not start for another week. You have not even met anybody yet other than the hired domestic help, except possibly one neighbour you already sense is worried you are going to be a pest. The slow burn begins. What do you do?

Not much, I am afraid, except to hit him up for as much spare cash as possible (since you are buying everything to settle into your new home and do not want to run short, especially in countries where only he has been allowed to open or have the bank account). Also secure a list of emergency phone numbers so you do not feel completely cut off in his absence. Steel yourself for his departure (which can often be that same evening) and tell yourself you are a big girl. And extract a promise from him that upon his return, he will be obliged to give you some free time to come back down to earth. If he leaves without making such a promise, proceed to unpack all the moving boxes except those containing his clothes, books, games, etc. and leave it for him to do. Hide his sporting equipment and tell him the movers lost that box. And plan your first getaway.

I Have to Work Late, Dear

Overtime will be an ongoing problem. The trick is to set certain conditions under which your spouse is positively prohibited from working late or bringing his work home because he can now (and once again, he is conveniently missing the hectic sup-per/bedtime "zero hour" around your house if children are involved). Show some flexibility except under the following cir-cumstances: birthdays, anniversaries, and other special occa-sions; particularly bad days for yourself that may coincide with the maid/amah/ayah's day off. Most important of all, *never* allow him to work late when *his* relatives are enjoying your hos-pitality in one of those month-long travel extravaganzas in which an in-law refuses to leave the house without you. In those cases, he should be forced to arrive home earlier than expected.

I do not intend to delve too deeply into serious marital prob-lems that arise overseas such as philandering with a local girl—which is, unfortunately, becoming more and more common and messy. I have written an entire book on the subject of expa-triate marriage that includes a chapter entitled "When a Move-able Marriage Goes Wrong." However, when there have been too many late nights, it may be time to visit his office and gauge the office staff's reaction to your presence. Extreme embarrass-ment—that is, nobody will look you in the eye—should be your first clue that all is not kosher. Until there is something to suspect, give him the benefit of the doubt that he is indeed working hard. And if you really want to give him a hard time about it, try to have a single good-looking male neighbour from upstairs chatting cozily beside you over a drink when he finally does arrive home. That will get his juices going.

Wining and Dining Clients

An important client is in town without his wife, and your hus-band is responsible for his night-time entertainment. Working suppers at the hotel are one thing; a tour of every sleazy strip joint or girly bar your city may have to offer is something differ-ent. These late-night jaunts are often critical to the signing of a deal, so it is futile to put up too much of a fuss. The only practi-cal piece of advice I can offer was something suggested to me by a corporate wife in Taipei whose husband was on the late-night social whirl while she stayed at home wondering if he would make it home alive after a night of heavy drinking: Make sure he does not drive himself. If it means hiding the car keys that day or forgoing the use of the driver (if you have one) so he can work a late shift, the only comfort you can provide for yourself in these instances is to ensure his safety above all else. And put other worries to the back of your brain.

In some cases, your husband may tell you that wives are definitely not on the invitation list. Later, you find out that half the office staff was there, including that exotic, young, unmarried, locally hired secretary you have had bad dreams about. OK, maybe you are being paranoid, but after too many of those evenings, I would simply arrive uninvited and pay the consequences. Just because you are paranoid does not mean you should not be.

Weekend Rounds of 'Work-Related' Golf

This is a particularly thorny issue with men. How thorny? When I was living in Taipei, I was asked to write a column for spouses in a magazine produced for the local chapter of the American Chamber of Commerce. I chose the subject of golf.

"There's a four-letter word which is driving women crazy," I wrote, "and it doesn't begin with the letter 'f'. It ends with it." Very funny and well-written was the reaction from the director at the time. "But," he said, "no way it can appear in print. I will offend our members." I was censored.

In my mind, golf is a leisure activity, no matter which way you swing the club. Strolling leisurely down a fairway and stopping for beers afterwards beats dragging the children through a chaotic traffic jam to the local swimming pool for lessons or watching while a half-dozen playmates of your child trash your house all afternoon in an effort to keep everyone occupied on a non–school day. That is invariably the wife's Saturday-afternoon scenario while the husband "unwinds" and talks business over a casual round on the links.

I am not advocating a complete ban on weekend sports, since they obviously promote good health, both mental and physical. But the rules of fair play should be applied to the domestic situation. Set limits on the number of rounds per month. You are allowed leisure time too, especially on weekends. All those family amusements should be shared overseas because they are often difficult to get to, if they even exist.

Forced-Upon Social Occasions

"Just this once, please. I don't ask for much." He is begging you to go with him to a cocktail party where you know with complete certainty there will likely be no other females (or very few) and nobody will be speaking English.

"Forget it. Absolutely not."

A two-hour argument ensues, which naturally you do not and cannot win. So you go, only to discover that there are in fact no other females and nobody speaks English. You turn right around and walk out the door, ignoring all attempts at an apology. You let your phone ring and ring and let him sweat about your safety. It takes you about twelve hours to let the resentment ooze out of your pores.

Second scenario: Dinner for twelve people, twelve strangers connected entirely with his work, who would sure love some home cooking since they have been on the road for a while. You have to do all the main cooking but your maid/amah/ayah is still needed in the kitchen and cannot possibly be spared for child-related duties. There is still so much to do, especially as you have been given less than a day's notice to prepare. The children need to be bathed and put to bed before the guests arrive. Who could possibly be free to handle that task?

Your husband arrives home early enough but "I have to have this report read by tomorrow," he whines, "and this time before the guests arrive will be my only chance. Can't you put the kids to bed, dear?"

"Is that before or after I ruin the dinner?"

If that comment does not work, I suggest immediate strike action. Let him make his own dinner party at a restaurant.

Doctor Disasters

In some overseas assignments a simple visit to the doctor can become a challenge. Never mind that half the time you are unsure of the competency of the local medical profession, to say nothing of abrupt bedside manners that can leave you convinced you are dying of some unnamed (or garbled by a heavy local accent) disease. Just getting to a hospital can sometimes require half a day's commitment. Finding a parking spot when you get there takes the rest of the day.

In short, hospital or doctor's visits can be a nightmare. And just for once, you would prefer either some help with the expedition or possibly the opportunity to turn the responsibility over to your husband, who has only heard second-hand tales of the experience.

Emergencies are never planned. Inoculations, on the other hand, are scheduled, so they lend themselves to a sharing of responsibility around appointments. Knowing well enough ahead of time when the third injection of whatever childhood vaccination is to take place means your husband can clear his schedule well in advance to take junior to the doctor.

But when the day arrives, he cannot make it. No regrets. Either a barefaced lie: "You never told me about this appointment," or a dodge: "Something more important has come up." In either event, your blood pressure is boiling. Might as well see the doctor yourself while you are there. Next time, write down the day and time of the appointment with your lipstick all over his best shirt or car windshield. Remind him that the children have two parents and one of them is consistently too busy to look after them.

Career Disputes

Of all the issues that breed resentment overseas, the pursuit of career goals by the female half of an expatriate couple runs the highest risk for ongoing battles and bitterness. Even women who are pursuing so-called mobile careers can work up a good sweat over this issue.

What causes a woman's career resentment? It is not a question of salary, as most work obtained overseas by a travelling wife rarely yields enough money to pay the grocer. More probably, it is a wife's resentment that she is wasting time professionally, or her sheer frustration at trying to do anything that is not fraught with hassle because it is being attempted overseas. Add to that some of a wife's own guilt about being out of the workforce—and perhaps even enjoying it if she is not frustrated about it—and you find a woman just looking for a good fight.

Women want to work for reasons other than money, many of which I explored in chapter 5. They include more than a desire to ensure she does not lose track, literally, of her place in the professional world she has chosen for herself. Some women simply do not want their brain to turn to mush if they can help it. Working provides stimulation and the opportunity to enhance oneself, which raising children, as cute as they are, does not offer completely.

It is challenging enough to find work overseas that is stimulating and compatible with a woman's skills, so when a husband reins in her efforts, very often for absolutely and purely selfish reasons ("I don't want you working. I want you at home with the children"), a wife's resentment levels can cross new thresholds. "Don't they need a father too?" you will likely ask to no avail as he heads for his office.

If you want to work, and your husband is holding you back without good reason, you may have very serious marital problems brewing that can only be alleviated by constant communication and re-evaluation of your life together. If it is all right for him to be compulsive about his career, you are allowed to be too.

If it is an embassy or company or the government of the foreign country you are temporarily residing in that is holding you back because of lack of a work permit, this is a serious problem. Short of your husband changing jobs, you are out of both luck and the job market. Try to be mature enough to take such obstacles in your stride.

But worst of all and worth screaming at the top of your lungs over is the husband who patronizes your initiative or displays a lack of understanding about any efforts you may be making on your own professional behalf. There you are, working independently on some lifelong project (a book perhaps?) or freelance consulting at anything possible and your entire working infrastructure may depend on maids to do translation, phone numbers that do not work, dangerous taxi rides to get to an appointment, or lengthy waiting periods for minimal payments. And there sits your husband, in a fancy local office, with staff coming and going to arrange all his appointments, drive him to them, and other office support systems. Go ahead. It is not hard to resent him. You are not alone in feeling that way.

Difficult as it is to rise above these feelings, you must if you are to go the distance of the posting together. Your working environment will not be the same as his, and the sooner you realize this, the less frustrated you will feel. Remember that you do not need to answer to some idiot back in headquarters on the other side of the world. That is just one of your husband's headaches. By all means leave him to it.

Transportation Trauma

Getting from place to place in some foreign cities can often be the most formidable problem you will face on a daily basis. Traffic jams and overcrowded buses are a familiar sight. Many women enjoy the security and luxury of drivers, while others slog it out behind the wheel themselves or take their chances with taxis.

If you get used to the safety and security of a chauffeur-driven car, you will be thrown into a panic when your husband informs you that you will have to go without the car while some out-of-town big shot enjoys your perquisite, especially if this news coincides with the week you have made several appointments for yourself and the children. The office will always take precedence over you, remember that, and that is one reason why from the very beginning, transportation should be negotiated between yourself and your husband.

Try not to agree to use the office car and driver for personal use, since this will invite (and rightly so) interference and changes to plans. Try to secure a vehicle that is your own to drive and the use of which cannot be challenged. If that is not feasible economically, then budget for taxis and buses and learn well in advance how to use them.

If you blindly agree to use only the office transportation when it is convenient, you can be sure that on the day you need it desperately, it will not be available to you. Sure, you will resent your husband, but the situation is really your own bad planning and laziness. This is one area of resentment that can be avoided.

About Our Holiday, Dear

You have waited and now you are just hours away from a weekend getaway—just the two of you. It has been so long since you were alone together you can hardly remember the experience. The children have been briefed, the help is in place, the reservations are made, and then hubby phones home from the office and calls the whole thing off in a matter of seconds. The boss needs him because some last-minute visitor from headquarters has arrived in town.

"I need you too. We need to get away," you say. "Sorry, maybe next time." He hangs up his phone. You throw yours against the wall. The same thing happens several months later for almost the same reasons. The boss has some mystical hold on your husband

(and his career) and cannot be antagonized, not for your sake anyway. Hold your resentment and anger. Your husband is probably feeling so guilty about cancelling that his emotions alone are enough for your marriage to handle at one time. There will be other weekends. However, if he consistently cancels, tell him you are going away with the cute guy from upstairs and then see how much the boss needs him.

Home Leave Alone

To some expatriate women, the shock would probably kill them if their husbands *did* in fact come home with them. They are so used to travelling around the world alone with children and parcels and luggage, and crying on airplanes from exhaustion, and fighting with in-laws from tension, and on and on, that if their husband has promised to come along one year and then cancels on them at the last minute, this will likely be taken in stride along with the rest of the emotional traumas just described.

Home leave, alone or with a partner, is definitely one of those areas one should always be prepared to grit one's teeth over and steel one's emotions against in the face of an onslaught of family, food, and fatigue. In this way, if your husband bolts at the last minute, your health does not suffer. You are already a mess just from the thought of all that psychological terrorism.

But when you are actually cruising at thirty thousand feet over a major body of water with two children who refuse to go to sleep no matter what medicine you pump into their bodies, that is the time to seethe with resentment and anger. Take a deep breath and remind yourself that everyone gets through it somehow and that it is only once a year. And then conveniently forget to buy him what he wants or needs.

Posting Time Again

If anything can be learned from my tales of guilt and resentment contained in this book, it is this: when your husband says you are on the move again, experience should provide you with the information to ask intelligent questions about the next stop on the expatriate express.

Start from the first section and work your way downward. For example, if his working too late or too much fuels your resentment, make sure you know how much the next place will require his presence at the office late at night. Devise a point system for the ten areas I highlighted, and if the score runs too high, as in ten out of ten, where the situation will be a nightmare again, then use your common sense and refuse to budge. I am always willing to help soothe any women's distress if she accidentally walked into the situation that is causing her so much anxiety. But if she knew in advance just how perilous this situation was going to be, she has nobody to blame but herself if she agrees to move again. As a therapist once told me: "No is a complete sentence."

In Beijing, I became part of a women's support group (some of the husbands called it the "Women in Trouble" group in a complete misunderstanding of its purpose). One subject that roused heated conversation and debate was the option for travelling women to simply say no to their husbands about yet another move or to have veto power over the choice of a world capital. I fell into the camp who decided that not only could women say no, they should positively refuse to agree to a move they know will be dissatisfying for them. There are no absolute answers and readers can hold their own arguments over this issue.

A Defense for the Husband

Yes, in the interest of fairness, I am going to attempt to offer a defense for expatriate husbands, starting with a reminder that upon your arrival, your husband is just as tired, jet-lagged and culture shocked as you are. With input from my own husband

(I could not have thought up the following rationalizations entirely on my own), I am going to momentarily give the expatriate husband the benefit of the doubt. This exercise should serve the dual purpose of showing what a fair-minded woman I am and also assist overseas wives in critically assessing their resentment. It also allows me the opportunity to throw cold water over any argument a man may raise in his own defense.

I will begin with the most important consideration. After reading all of the issues I have just raised which can cause resentment to grow overseas, ask this question: Do many of these same issues happen at home too? Or have they suddenly cropped up in a foreign country?

Corporate animals, those living and breathing by the words of the chief executive officer, do not suddenly appear fully formed after a long flight overseas. They often take years to develop and were likely around back home. Many wives should not be surprised when they move abroad and find their husband has become a maniac about his work in the new setting too. If he is working long hours overseas, he probably was doing the same thing before you left to live abroad. A wife should not blame her husband for changing overnight, when she may always have been living with a driven workaholic all along. Marriage problems do not vanish when you change location, although many people would like that to be so and move in an attempt to accomplish just that.

Of course, back home, where you understood the language, the infrastructure was solid, friends and family provided support systems, and you yourself may have had a professional identity and well-paying job, it was a little easier to let your husband be driven by his career ambitions.

Defense Number Two: it is a fact that for many expatriates, overseas life often provides such perquisites as household help to assist you with children, drive you around chaotic cities, and keep your yard clear of leaves or other rubbish. Many households, depending on where you are posted, have enough people on hand to make sure the expatriate couple do little but enjoy the overseas life.

When a woman starts resenting her husband's long working hours, naturally he will remind her of just how much staff she has at her disposal or how his work is the very reason you are all overseas. He will push his guilt, if he has any, out of his mind about habitually missing the supper hour with his children because, after all, the maid is there to do everything. "Why should my wife complain?" he will say to his friends.

In situations where it is affordable and easy to come by, it is indeed true that household help carries a great load for expatriate couples. I mean, why should anyone bother to fold a shirt and put it away when it can be left on the floor where one drops it, to be washed, ironed, and neatly tucked away in the drawer? That may have been all right for the male imperialists of centuries gone by, but in the twenty-first century, the formerly serving classes are now part of the new emerging industrialized nations of the world.

Many expatriate working men who are essentially the lord and master of their kingdoms at the office, with local staff members doing everything but kissing their rings, conveniently lose sight of this global view. They abdicate all family responsibilities to their low-paid serfs in the mistaken belief that these helpers still serve as surrogate parents, which was often the case in colonial days.

In the diplomatic service, when a man starts taking himself and his inflated overseas position too seriously, it is believed he is suffering from "Ambassador Syndrome." A man starts to seriously believe that he is, in fact, His Excellency, and manual labour, like giving his son or daughter a bath, is too much beneath him.

His Excellency must simply be reminded from time to time that back in the real world where he comes from, he is simply Mr. Ordinary Joe, and his serving minions will vanish the minute he leaves his job, along with his money (or foreign passports) to hand out. He better remember how to do things for himself, because if he does not, he may not have a wife and family on his return.

A third defense for the expatriate male: the foreign culture can be blamed for turning him into the monster you claim he has become. This argument definitely has more validity than the other two I just mentioned. It is hard to say no to a local counterpart whose culture, towards women at any rate, may lag centuries behind your own. It is true that many of us come from societies with expectations of equality in the raising of our families that just do not exist in other cultures. Japan is a good example of a highly industrialized country in which men spend about as much time on their families as a woman spends in the bath each day.

An expatriate man may be trying to satisfy his clients, who expect behaviour similar to their own, in which case a man is literally caught between a rock and a hard place. Any way he turns, he is bound to annoy either party. He can risk saying no to his company (usually at the risk of his career), but he can rarely say no to a client. A wife has to understand these cultural and corporate parameters and curb her resentment and anger if she can.

But Given All These Excuses...

Despite the pressure being placed on the husband by his work, the raison d'être for your life overseas, there are many steps he can take to alleviate some of the resentment they encourage. It is often up to the wife to suggest the following:

- Together, you and your husband must designate time each day for one another (and not just saying good-night). For instance, a husband can leave fifteen minutes later for the office in the morning to allow for a cup of coffee together where nothing controversial is discussed. Talk about anything else, future plans, the weather, sports (ice hockey has worked for me), a book, but make time for each other and communicate.

- Make a date for lunch once a week or a dinner out together alone one evening where you face each other across the table without the distraction of other people or children. Neither party is allowed to cancel.
- If you cannot get away on a trip, a local hotel room can be booked overnight and a babysitter back home, allowing you a quiet night together and breakfast alone in the morning. These twelve-hour getaways have proven most effective in many marriages.
- Try not to let situations get too inflamed before sitting down to hammer them out. Often women are their own worst enemies in letting situations slide until they are too far gone. At the first sign of confrontation, get it out in the open and clear the air.
- Plan your own private retreat with other women or by yourself, to a spa, a famous tourist site, or perhaps a professional development conference being held in the region. These solo trips are critical to your mental health, so make sure you do them when opportunities present themselves.

All of these suggestions are not beyond the realm of possibility and should be attempted, especially when you live overseas and the day-to-day tension of life in a foreign culture diminishes your powers of patience.

Resenting Your Children
Feelings of resentment towards your children are much harder to own up to than those you may habour towards your mate. You will be sitting around with a group of women openly confessing that you wish your children would just vanish for a few days. These are secret resentment scenarios. You feel guilty if your children's health is endangered by poor medical facilities

or a polluted environment, resentful if childcare does not measure up to the quality you may have enjoyed at home.

I will be the first to admit to resenting my children at various times. When we first arrived on our posting to Taiwan and my son was barely two and so culture shocked he pushed me close to the edge of my sanity, I was constantly torn between my unconditional love for him and my fantasy of walking out the door and doing what I wanted to do, instead of babysitting a screamer.

Daycare was invented for a certain kind of mother, and I would be lying if I did not confess to being one of them. When my children were small, I still desperately needed to have some part of my day to myself to pursue my own interests and career goals. I cannot hide this fact. Like a lot of women, I am also torn between the media myth of a superwoman and my own reality.

It is natural to have these feelings of resentment. While I do not suggest you tell your children this fact outright, I used to have long conversations with my own about the direct relationship between their mother's mood and her opportunities to have some quiet time to work. I found that talking about it actually muted some of my resentment towards them, and at the same time, subliminally taught them a few life lessons for later. We all need our time and space—including their mother.

The challenge has always been to come face to face with your child's needs and your own, then work your way around them without resentment and blind fury getting in the way. It took me years as a parent, but I finally dealt with my feelings by accepting them and decided to let each day unfold by itself. Some days I could work, others were just impossible. When those latter days arose, I just faced up to it and spent the day at the park wherever we were living in the world.

The guilt you may face by bringing children to an unhealthy environment altogether is one that is much tougher to reconcile. It also fuels fights with your husband, because of course it is *his* fault you are living in a country that gives your daughter asthma or whatever the local disease may be.

When we moved to Taipei, my daughter spent almost three months with a nagging, phlegm cough that made her sound like a heavy smoker, which at the age of six, she definitely was not. The local doctors dismissed the cough with this typical diagnosis: It was the cough all foreign children got because of the pollution. In my daughter's situation, that was not the case, but we only discovered this after we medically evacuated her to Hong Kong and saw a specialist. It turned out she had a common dust allergy, not unlike one I suffer from, and we were able to set her on course. Naturally, I instantly blamed Taiwan for giving my daughter the allergy, until the doctor patiently explained that she was going to have it anywhere we lived, although polluted Taipei did not improve it.

Your children are going to come down with many childhood diseases regardless of where you are living, so it is pointless to feel guilty over their bad health. If they do come down with something that the local environment is most definitely making much worse (asthma for instance), then it is a fair request to make sure your husband works fast at moving you out of there. But do not feel guilty over something you cannot possibly control.

Another guilt trip endemic to moving children around the world, especially teenagers, is feeling that you have taken them from their friends and believing them when they shout at you that you have ruined their life forever. Children say this a lot, especially teenagers, and quite naturally know which guilt strings to pull. In these situations, wait until six months have gone by and your child is truly settled. Chances are they will have found so many new friends that the memories of the old ones will begin to fade. The long-term advantages you are giving your children by moving them around the world will eventually outweigh adolescent outbursts.

And Now for the Real Guilt

A more straightforward guilt that will be easier to pinpoint will be the guilt you feel should you be posted to a poverty-stricken developing country. While you are busy complaining about drivers or maids or the quality of the curtains in the family room, outside your gates, women and children are living a marginal existence in some moth-eaten shelter with barely enough to eat. Those husbands are not out working long hours. They have simply vanished, often into prison or a faraway province in search of work, leaving the mother to raise their six or more children by herself without any support system at all and without any financial resources except her two strong hands.

Have I made you feel guilty yet? You should, so count your blessings every day of the week. I am not trying to trivialize all of the preceding discussion about what a creep your husband can be, but when you take time to compare your situation to the desperate lives of half of the world's population, you gain a new perspective on your own "problems."

Remember that you are travelling to see how the other half of the world lives, and often it is not a pretty sight. You are insulated and protected with an expatriate life. If you think that life is letting you down, look out your window and pack up your extra baggage, guilt, and resentment. Try to channel that energy into helping the people with whom you are sharing the scenery. Your guilt and resentment will quickly vanish and you will perhaps in the process improve someone else's life, even just a little bit.

10 Going Home
Return Shock

The shock of going home will depend a lot on how long you have been away, but absolutely everyone, regardless of the length of their posting, will feel some jolt from the changes to her environment. That is the nature of any kind of adjustment period and forms the essence of what has been identified by researchers as "return shock": the adjustment period to unexpected changes in the people you know; the places you lived; the events you have missed; and the unexpected changes in yourself, both emotionally and physically.

My first re-entry experience after three years in Thailand offered me its share of jolts. The biggest shock of all was feeling like an outsider in my own culture. While I lived in Bangkok, I was used to feeling like an alien because I was one; in Canada, I should have felt right at home but instead I felt totally disconnected and left out of the mainstream. My cultural reference points were out of date because we lived abroad before the Internet could keep us up to date on changes to the pop culture. I had nothing current to contribute to a conversation: the biggest shock of all for a constant talker like myself!

One of my strongest shocks occurred at a Toronto Blue Jays baseball game. The cheering crowd jumped to its feet to execute the "wave." I thought it was absolutely wonderful and unique and could not stop laughing until my companions regarded me strangely with that "Where've you been? Outer space?" look. I took my seat, the smile wiped from my face. I would barely venture another cheer and chose instead to stuff my face with mystery meat hot dogs and doughy pretzels. It felt like I had really landed from Mars, not from Southeast Asia. I did not just feel completely out of it. I was.

The good news in this scenario, though, is that like its counterpart, straightforward country culture shock, return shock is not fatal. You get over it, especially if you can laugh about it, and not just in a hysterical, over-the-edge kind of way. You do eventually catch up on people and events. It truly helps, though, if you know what to watch for.

The Challenges of Returning

Some expatriates positively fear the idea of going home and avoid it all costs, especially if they think they might return to home base and never get out in the world again. As a foreign service family, we were luckier: it is part of the rotational life to be returned home for a two- or three-year assignment before taking another posting abroad. Knowing that returning home is part of your international life cycle means you can build contingency plans into your routine, such as owning a house back in your own country, which allows you to take up residence in the same neighbourhood each time you are posted home.

Returning to your own familiar neighbourhood can help soften one of the major shocks of re-entry, which is the strain of stepping back into a strange setting in your own country. Unlike your posting abroad, there will be no community centre or built-in support system waiting to brief you on local life, prices, and culture. You are expected to know these things. You are from that country, after all, even if the neighbourhood is new and the absence of support groups can make you feel extremely isolated at the beginning.

Travelling and living in a country profoundly different from your own cannot help but alter your outlook on life. You may look upon your old institutions and organizations with a new perspective, which is not always very positive. We tend to idealize our country while we are away, and when we return and find our own society riddled with problems, or unappreciative of just how well-off we are compared to other countries, it tends to encourage cynicism and bad feelings all round.

You want to shout at your old friends and neighbours that they are exceedingly well off. They look at your outbursts askance, than carry on complaining about the price of an SUV or the latest BlackBerry model. So you may regard your friends in a new light, which may not be so glowing. They have changed too, but you feel your change has been more dramatic, leading to a tendency to dismiss anything that may have happened in their lives. Once again, you feel alienated from your old circle of friends and acquaintances, and feel even more disconnected from your new home environment.

Family can pose another problem, especially if an aging parent has been cared for by a sibling who looks at you upon return and says: "OK, now it's your turn to look after our mother. I've done it for three years and I'm taking a break now that you're back." You feel barely capable of organizing your own family's life, and suddenly there is filial duty beckoning.

Careers may be re-evaluated by your new, internationally enlightened persona. I made a complete career change upon returning to Canada from Thailand. Before I left home, I had been a broadcast journalist. When I returned and unpacked my old television reporter clothes (which admittedly after the birth of my daughter could not fit over my expanded body), I instantly threw them in a pile for the Salvation Army.

Those clothes fit a woman who just did not exist anymore. I looked at myself critically in the mirror and did not see the former television reporter staring back at me. Far from being tailored and professional looking, my hair was wild looking; I had toned down my makeup almost to nothing since I had been permanently tanned from the tropical Thai sun, and my glasses (previously horn-rimmed academic-looking frames) were now bright pink. Who would possibly hire me now, I thought, except for a travelling circus? Granted, I fell back temporarily into freelancing for the more anonymous radio service (I had to make some money, after all), but I knew there was no going back to the kind of professional television person I used to be.

Children are especially vulnerable when they return home and require more than the usual attention in order to settle into new schools and new routines. The Internet has made it easier to keep up with cultural touchstones, but if they are entering junior or senior high school, when peer pressure to conform is at its greatest, their feelings of alienation can set off all sorts of adjustment problems and depression. Your husband, too, may need your support and common sense to see him through the transition. The changes in his working environment and status may easily unravel him in the beginning.

As the wife and mother, you must deal with all of your family's issues while simultaneously unpacking, decorating, stocking up, renovating, and a thousand and one other responsibilities that in combination will give you sleepless nights. Your own life is put on hold until you get your family settled, and that may depress you if you are anxious to get onto something new. Still, just as there are many challenges to re-entry, so too are the number of solutions, which I will deal with later in this chapter. And a reminder: since the publication of this book, I have written an entire volume devoted solely to the subject of repatriation called *Homeward Bound: The Spouse's Guide to Repatriation.*

There's No Place Like Home

Before getting down to the challenges one by one, however, I feel it is important to stress that while many negative factors will be at work during your first months back, there are also many positive feelings to be savoured. Certainly there will be drawbacks to being home, but do not forget for one minute the advantages and sweetness of being home.

The day we drove up the lane to our house, soon after our return from Thailand, through the pine trees, past the duck pond, and up the hill to where the house we owned at the time sat on a wide open meadow, fronted by a panoramic view of the Gatineau Hills outside of Canada's capital city, Ottawa, my breath and heart literally stopped. It was so beautiful. There was barely a sound other than the wind—a clean, sweet-smelling wind to distract us. Wildflowers were blooming around the house and in the meadow. The grass (we had not seen real grass in years) was freshly cut in a fringe around our acre of land. I wanted to cry I was so happy to be home. I was also so relieved that we had not made a mistake in buying so swiftly that even with my hay fever, I wanted to kiss the goldenrod.

It is true that we sometimes tend to falsely idealize our home countries during an overseas assignment. Exasperated by an alien environment and climate, we delude ourselves into thinking there is no place in the world as clean, as organized, as crime-free, as poverty-free, as picture perfect as our country of birth. It is wrong to paint such a false picture without running the risk of complete disillusionment when we return home. But at the same time, there is no law against truly cherishing and certainly not dismissing the small things that can make going home such a touching experience.

Re-Entry Is a Three-Step Process

Think of your return home as an experience that will have three distinct stages. The first obvious step will be to let go of the past. This is known as the "closure" stage. You are not only closing up a house or apartment at a post, you are closing up your overseas life as well. It is crucial that you feel like you have closed a door (in preparation of opening another) in order to know that part of your life is truly over, leaving only memories to linger in your mind—not deeds or goodbyes left half-done. For that reason, make sure you say all your farewells. Do not disappear out of town. Try to do all the things you never got around to doing, like visiting a spectacular tourist site or museum. Allow your children to say goodbye completely by scheduling sleepovers with friends or organizing their own farewell parties at school or at home.

Try to get everything done within four days of your departure so you can relax and take a few deep breaths before heading out to the airport. Similarly, try not to mentally leave a place too early. If you have moved in your mind three months before your physical departure, that can be unhealthy as well. Try to balance out your time doing something each day until your departure date while allowing some quiet time before beginning the trek home. Being organized helps but do not worry that you have lists all over the place. Do what I did before moving abroad my second time. I pasted notes all over my house with the words "DON'T PANIC" to keep myself from hyperventilating.

The second stage of returning home is the turmoil or crazy period when you are neither here nor there. It is part of the process of disconnecting and can bring with it feelings similar to the anger and depression you felt when you first went abroad. You are out of control again. Perhaps you are "home" but living out of a suitcase, camping out in a parent's spare bedroom or hotel suite.

This is the unsettled time, when the previous life has ended but the new one at home has not settled into any recognizable pattern as of yet. You may still be travelling, or at home renovating and fixing up your house. Your days are filled with checking out new schools, finding activities for toddlers, buying new cars or furniture, or attending to the million and one details of moving into a new environment.

The trip back to your own country may be behind you, but there are still many miles to go mentally until you have truly arrived home. Think of this stage as one of uncertainty. Do not expect instant routines. Give yourself a break emotionally and do not expect too much too fast. Remember that Rome was not built in a day and all those other clichés that always contain a kernel of truth.

The third and final phase of the re-entry process is the period of reconnection. The house is livable again, your furniture has arrived, the kids are back at school, and finally you have a minute to yourself to think about what you may want to do.

I remember so clearly when this phase arrived for me on my first re-entry. Then two-year-old Lilly was settling into a new babysitting situation; the house had furniture even if more pieces were required. Rodney had returned to a headquarters job, and I sat in a shopping mall enjoying a coffee, that day's morning newspaper (not one three or four weeks out of date), and a glorious bran muffin, something I had not tasted in three years.

The satisfaction I received from the bran muffin alone came close to euphoria. I wanted to cry I felt so happy to be back in Canada. Never mind that I did not know what I was going to do. I enjoyed the fleeting moment of satisfaction of being home just as the leaves were changing colour, the air was crisp, and the unpolluted sky was the brightest of blues.

The Issues You Will Face
Still, when the bran muffin was eaten, the coffee drunk to the last drop, and the newspaper read from cover to cover, I was faced with a reality not unlike the "Now what?" syndrome I described in an earlier chapter. Just as I had to get on with my life overseas and not mope around, now that I was home in Canada, I had to get on with my life again. There were issues that Rodney and I had to face head-on, such as my working again (or not), worry over money for mortgage payments and renovations, and the impact of losing inexpensive household help, to name three big ones, that we could no longer postpone discussing.

Flying Money
Your foreign money, the kind whose exchange rates seemed as enigmatic as the people on the streets back at post, goes into the drawer for future trips. The time arrives to confront the new budget. Sure, you started to think in your local currency the moment you stepped off the plane, but now the bills are being

totalled up, and both you and your husband can no longer avoid the complete and horrifying fiscal panic of being home.

While fixing up our new house on our first re-entry, I had joked with my husband that our money had taken wing and could be seen soaring over the hills of our new panoramic view. It was flying at a fast and furious pace. Appliances, carpets, cars, daycare, groceries, warm clothes . . . the expenses went on and on. So did our "budget discussions," usually in an atmosphere so tense we could have marketed it for a new form of energy. We were horrified at the new controls we had no choice but to impose on our lifestyle. We had a mortgage for the first time in our lives, taxes, and all sorts of hidden costs to home ownership no one could possibly have prepared us for.

Watching money fly is a popular post–expatriate life game, except no one is enjoying it because in the real world there are no cost-of-living allowances that allowed you that fantasy life back at post. Nobody is helping you adjust to your new high cost of living now, and the price of everything, and everything you seem to need to buy at once, reduces you to many stormy sessions with your spouse. Worse, you cannot complain to anyone, because your friends figure you have made a fortune overseas and lived the good life long enough.

The best you can do under your new restraints is to draw up a budget. Set priorities on your needs and expectations for the coming year and allot existing funds, what may be left of your savings, to those needs. Make sure your budget is based on sound price surveys. Be realistic. You cannot cut yourself off from life completely. That would be as extreme as going on a 700 calorie a day diet.

A Decision a Day . . .

Another popular game for returning expatriates is called decision overload. How many critical decisions can you try to make in a single day? Sometimes there can be so many decisions to be made at once that you spend as much time deciding on a new car as you spend on selecting salt and pepper shakers.

Decision-making cannot be helped on re-entry. In your hurry to get everyone settled and some semblance of order restored as quickly as possible, you want all the pieces of your new life to fall together in the fastest possible time. This encourages hasty decision-making and lumping too many crucial decisions, ones you would normally take weeks to make, in the space of hours instead of weeks.

New furniture and cars seem to get quick nods from a lot of returning expatriates. Under normal circumstances, price surveys, consumer reports, and other information would be gathered. Not so in the case of a returning family. Research flies out the window, and so does good taste. Be aware that this could happen to you, and put the brakes on the minute you feel yourself playing the game too much in earnest. A half-empty house filled with furniture you like, as opposed to ugly stuff you picked out too quickly, will be a happier home in the end. The same applies to a car worth its money. Take a deep breath and try to look before you leap.

No Support System

For those who had household help while overseas, you will feel a kind of panic erupting when you realize the help you relied on overseas did not come home in the shipment. *How can I manage my household?* you wonder frantically, forgetting you did it for many years before enjoying the luxury of help, whom you have also conveniently forgotten may have driven you crazy. I was so relieved to be *without* help in the house on returning to Canada that I joyfully cleaned toilets and vacuumed away my first few weeks. I cannot guarantee this feeling will continue, but the point to be made here is that you are not as helpless as you think. When you moved abroad, you were also well taken care of for the first few weeks by another company wife, or embassy official, or perhaps a professional orientation organization. Your questions were answered, sympathy was ministered, and emotionally you felt others understood how you were feeling and you took comfort from that.

The absence of this life support system on returning home can at first leave you feeling helpless and without resources. Yes, this can be jarring, but getting used to your own country all over again will not be as hard as adjusting to another, even if it seems formidable at first. After all, people speak your language at home. And friends who may have momentarily been confused by the new you will come around. They are your friends. Do not be afraid to ask them for help.

Your Children's Safety

Overseas, your children were never far from your watchful eye. At home, suddenly they want to hang out in the local mall with their pals or ride their bike in a busy street. As a mother, your heart goes into your throat at the thought of their new-found independence, which they could not enjoy overseas.

It is natural to find these fears bubbling to the surface when you re-enter your old society. How you control them will be up to the individual, but at least acknowledge those fears will be there—and some for very good reasons, depending on the city you return to. But you cannot tie a rope to your children, especially if they are teenagers. All you can hope is that the common sense you ground into them will prevail.

How Not to Buy in Bulk

I heard a wonderful story of an expatriate returnee whose first grocery shopping trip, to fill her cupboards with staples and such, produced a whopping bill when she finally managed to steer her shopping carts (yes, multiple carts) to the checkout counter. Examining the high price of her goods, she realized she had bought dozens of everything, instead of the typical amounts one normally would buy for a week or two.

She was still in "home leave shopping mode," that frenetic, grab-it-all, load-it-up style of consumer madness when you buy as much as possible at one time so it will last you several months overseas.

You are home now. All those goods will continue to be stocked on the shelves at reasonably stable prices. There is no need to stockpile in case of famine or siege. Make a list before you go shopping and reasonably assess your family's needs under the new conditions. Another good idea when rebalancing the grocery budget under returnee austerity programs is to make a list of each night's meals for a week or two and buy only what you will need for those lunches or suppers. The same control should be applied to department stores. No need to buy two dozen cotton undies at once or a year's supply of expensive makeup. You can go back to the store again.

I have known expatriate couples who claim they can never go home again because without household help to pick up the pieces of their lives every day, meaning their pieces of discarded clothing, their marriages would fail to survive more than a day. For some couples, this fear is not totally without grounds.

Men get used to having constant help not only to assuage their guilt over running off to the golf course every weekend, but also to keep their wives happy without the burden of cleaning toilets. Women get used to having a jack-of-all-trades handy in the house to do everything from babysit to sew a button back on a jacket. And let us not forget all that ironing! For their part, children enjoy having a "neutral" third party to run to in the event of disagreements with their parents.

If household help has also been used as daycare, family budgets will also have to be readjusted to cope with the shock of finding out what daycare costs back home. How you adjust to a life without help will depend a lot on your personality. In my own case, I was relieved beyond belief not to have someone always hovering in the background, quietly manipulating me into decisions, making me feel completely useless as mother and homemaker, and leading me into scores of other emotional traumas I have worked hard to forget. This is not the case for everyone. If your return home with toddlers is to a four-bedroom house that needs a lot of cleaning, be prepared to have the most exhausting of return shocks. You will become a Molly Maid in suburban wherever, trapped within the walls of your house, mop in hand, tears rolling down your face from the exhaustion of re-entering the domestic labour force.

Remember that there are people known as cleaning ladies and there are also cleaning services that can be called in once in a while; there are home daycare centres; and there is your husband, whose job at home may not call him away as much nor require his presence every evening at a cocktail reception. Before you get totally overwhelmed by your new domestic lot, negotiate a new agreement, a "living at home, not abroad agreement," with your husband. And then place an ad in the local paper for the cheapest available help.

On the other hand, those returning to home countries where help is plentiful will feel the sweet relief of having help once again to peel, slice, chop, cook, mop, sweep, clean, wash, iron, and babysit. Once again you will be able to enjoy waking up late, knowing that the breakfast is already prepared for the children. The laundry will be all done, ironed and neatly put away, and you will not even have to handwash delicate lingerie yourself anymore. All the hassles of hiring good help and training them may go unnoticed when you first come home because all you can think of is that now someone else will be doing the chores you had to endure overseas.

Extended Family

You may think fondly of family when you are overseas, but your feelings can change dramatically when that same extended family is just round the corner or in the next town. All of the decisions and feelings you have been able to defer while being away will now come crashing down around you, just at the time when you need this the least, when you are in the throes of return shock. Your own problems of readjustment will seem insurmountable, but try loading those up with the problems of a sibling about to get divorced or an aging parent who requires hospitalization. Or just consider all the petty problems endemic to any typical family: the kind that will really make your blood boil especially if you have spent the last number of years in a poverty-stricken country. You will easily lose patience with family members complaining about their suburban neighbours who have an annoying dog, an unpainted fence, or uncut grass that your sibling complains is the blight of the neighbourhood.

Patience is a virtue. I have said it before, I will keep saying it. Your family simply does not understand where you are coming from and will be impatient with your limited interest in these so-called major problems that you just cannot get excited over.

Aging, ill parents, on the other hand, are a serious problem you cannot fly away from anymore, so be sure to preserve your best frame of mind for dealing with these more important issues. As for the rest of the so-called ills, try to laugh about them without alienating everybody. Do not engage in futile arguments where you bore everyone until their eyes glaze over from hearing about statistics of starving children or politically repressed citizens who would give their lives to live in neighbourhoods with uncut grass or half-painted fences. This does not do anybody any good, especially you. You are trying to reconnect with your family, not distance yourself even further.

The Boredom Factor

Where have all the interesting new people gone? Where are the fascinating visitors, the exotic side of life, the opportunities to experience something you have never seen or heard before? One of the major reasons a former expatriate will decide to return to the international life is the feeling that there is no excitement in sitting home in suburbia, watching the grass grow (only to be cut). There is a certain excitement to stepping on an airplane, passport in hand, flying off to an unknown destination, and facing the challenge of carving out a fulfilling life. There may be no such opportunities once you have moved home. You may feel, not long after you have settled in again, that you are itching to get away again. Many people do just that. They find another assignment and put this returning home idea off to the side for another decade.

But if there is no option—this is it, you are home to stay—at this point initiatives for participation and enthusiasm must be undertaken, even if at the beginning, your personal campaign to get excited is a little forced. This is the flip side of when you moved overseas and were advised to seek out opportunities both social and professional as quickly as possible. The same ambition must be mustered back home.

Nobody will hand you excitement or a new opportunity. The chance to branch out, even within a community you thought you knew inside out, exists if you know what you are looking for. Cultural societies abound in most cities but you may never have been looking for them before. There are Newcomers Clubs that have many rotational expat wives as members. Universities may offer courses related to the country you have just lived in. Antiques, art, music, ballet, theatre, and museums are all art forms and cultural institutions out there to offer points of contact if you are interested in keeping your mind open and you want to satisfy a craving to learn more about the country you just left. But you will not find these opportunities while staring out the window of your house into a deserted street.

The Humbled or Elevated Husband

Once you pull yourself or your children out of a return funk, you will likely be left facing your husband's letdown on being back at headquarters. His mood can affect the entire family. Overseas, he may have been riding high on his own self-importance to the point you wanted to throttle him once a day. Back at home, you are feeling sorry for him (as he is often feeling for himself) as you watch him go through the motions of a job that may not offer a tenth of the excitement and glamour of his overseas assignment. Instead of strutting out to work into a shiny overseas office or valiantly organizing the evacuation of flood victims in a remote village, he is standing on the bus clutching a strap with his briefcase held tightly between his knees. It can be a pathetic sight.

However, a good position back at headquarters may be a reward for a job well done abroad. If it is not, you can remind him (as often as necessary) that while overseas jobs can be glamorous and challenging, it is typically from headquarters that promotions and careers are made. Overseas, people tend to be forgotten, even if they are having the time of their lives. Your husband needs to be home for a while to network with the top people or just the ordinary middle managers who may hold the keys for future challenges. So while he may feel humbled momentarily, in the long run, he is doing his career a service by being back in the heart of the action.

In contrast to the humbled husband, your husband could have just returned from overseas after successfully completing his doctorate or an intensive training program. He returns home to discover that he has status now he has only dreamed about before. Most probably, he will be promoted and receive a much higher salary. Friends, neighbours, and relatives may even regard him with awe. You become the mate of a man whose feet have left the ground. Pull him back down before he floats away on a cloud of prestige.

How Not to Be the Misfit Family

There are obviously many things you should bear in mind when you are returning home from overseas after a long period. Here are few pointers on how to smooth out the transition from living overseas to living back home.

Plan ahead

Some experts on re-entry shock believe that planning for your return home should begin when you first move overseas. Obviously, it is difficult to think of coming home before you have even left, but you can do some planning, such as buying a house or renting out your own house to make sure you and your family return to the same neighbourhood. At your posting, there are a few measures you can take as well. One precaution we took against believing our own Raj-like lifestyle in Bangkok was driving that beat-up Canadian car I previously mentioned. I suppose it is terrific if you can afford a luxury car and driver, but remember that when you go home again, it may be back to economy cars. Try to keep a clear head on your shoulders. This will make it easier when you go back to your real world.

Temper expectations

Expectations can be deadly. Do not get it into your head that your home base will be perfect because it won't. Sometimes it is particularly easy to fall into this trap if you have not really enjoyed your overseas assignment. You convince yourself that back there at home is some suburban utopian crime-free society.

As I mentioned earlier, I had a horrible experience just prior to my return to Canada from Thailand that shook any idealized expectations I had of a safe world back home. One week before my daughter and I were scheduled to fly home to Canada, just the two of us, an Air India flight was blown out of the sky. The bomb originated in a Canadian airport, and a second bomb unfortunately detonated after landing on a flight to Tokyo that also started out in Canada.

So much for thinking home was going to be safe. Expectations about family can also be dangerous. Do not expect miracle reconciliations with family members you did not get along with before you left home.

Try not to re-enter alone

My flight home from Bangkok reminds me of another important piece of advice. Try to return home together. Often this is not possible, if your husband has work to finish up and you are anxious to grab the kids and be on your way, which was my own experience. Sure, you would love to escape, but getting to the other end and facing all the return shocks can be very hard on you emotionally.

Not only did travelling alone exhaust me beyond belief, but being without a partner with whom I could share all my return shock with—look at that green park, those empty streets, that loud-mouthed politician—was tough going. Unilateral decision-making is also difficult. It may pay to wait a few extra weeks to go home together.

Communicate

Before you leave and after you return, make sure the lines of communication between you and your children are not only open, but working overtime. Take your children to lunch before departure and hear out what they have to say about going home. Listen carefully to their expectations and apprehensions. Likewise, once you are home, listen to them some more. Do not get so wrapped up in picking out new wallpaper or carpeting that you do not hear them when they tell you they are scared, or tired all the time, or depressed. The same applies to your husband. Make sure you schedule time or conversation in between all that tying up of loose ends. During the chaotic time after you arrive home, try to get out to dinner or for a walk and check in with each other's feelings.

Attend to the special needs of children who re-enter

I cannot go into all the special emotional stroking your children will need (read *Homeward Bound* for more tips), but I can highlight a few areas to look out for. When it comes to decision-making, include your children wherever possible, especially if you are decorating a brand new room for them. Their bedrooms will become a safe haven, so make sure they are places they will enjoy bringing their new friends to. Find new activities for your children as a way of distracting them from their feelings of uprootedness. Sure, new activities require more effort and momentary feelings of alienation. But that is quickly replaced with new friends and new interests, which activities will encourage. Most of all, and especially if your children are teenagers, have a chat with their new teachers about not singling them out to talk about where they have just lived. Fitting in and seeming as normal as possible is a top priority for a teenager, so try to avoid a spotlight being cast on your child as the "kid who just returned from . . . "

See your country as a tourist

Another idea that works at bringing everyone up to date is to travel within your own country for a few weeks before settling it. This gives everyone a local/national focus again and provides conversation starters that do not necessarily deal with the country you have just returned from. Appreciate the cultural differences between home and abroad. Sure, there were things you probably will miss from your overseas home, but a local tour may help remind you of all the things you hated to leave in the first place.

Find others like yourselves

By this piece of advice, I do not mean that you should drop old friends because they have not travelled. But broaden your circle of friends to include people like yourselves who have lived expatriate lives. You can speak the same language and share your re-entry experiences.

Self-Confidence Does Return Eventually

Your self-confidence first vanished when you moved away. Now it vanishes again upon return. There is a contradiction at work here. On the one hand, your self-confidence may be overwhelming when it comes to subjects like foreign travel or the culture you enjoyed while away. On the other hand, you forget how to use a shopping centre or call up a maintenance person or plumber.

Trying to stay on an even keel in the way you view yourself can seem a daunting task at the beginning, but it can be done if you expect that wild mood swings will occur and plan appropriately. For instance, if you decide to go out and look for a job, do not do it on a day you have just freaked out over your inability to cope with childcare all over again. Wait for a day you can secure a babysitter and have a few minutes alone before rushing into someone's office all flustered and hysterical. Nobody is going to hire you in that state.

From my own experience, I found my self-confidence level soared when I returned briefly to my old profession as a free-lance journalist. What had been unbelievably difficult to carry out in Bangkok, a simple assignment foiled by useless telephones, transportation nightmares, hassle factors that measured right off the scale, became easy back home. It did not matter to me what an editor asked me to do when I discovered I could easily phone up someone for an interview (and an English-speaking person would answer the phone); I could drive to my appointment myself in traffic that was humanly safe; and the hassles were so limited I felt almost giddy.

It Can Take a Full Cycle of Seasons to Reintegrate

Certainly after six months you will begin to feel like your old self, but some people believe that it can take up to eighteen months to two years before you feel "at home." Not everyone will need that much time. Some may feel settled after just one cycle of seasons, which you can measure by the major holidays and festivals. You will not feel like you are really home until you have had your first Thanksgiving and Christmas back, your first Easter, May long and July long weekend, New Year's Day, National Day, Independence Day, or any other major holiday unique to your own country. When that cycle is complete, you will know you are home.

Give Yourself Time

Knowing that the re-entry experience requires a certain amount of time for readjustments will go a long way to easing the transition from over there to over here. As I have been trying to stress throughout these pages, information is power, and the more you know about how you will feel (and how other people also feel), the more this knowledge will boost your sense of excitement and satisfaction over the experience and that of your family too.

Do not expect too much at once, and do not expect too much of yourself. These are the final words of self-taught wisdom I can offer, except to suggest that you keep this book within easy reach for your next international assignment, just to remind yourself that although it will not be easy, you *can* indeed make a huge success out of moving abroad. You are now part of an international community of soul mates, who share the common, universal experiences of surviving—and thriving—in an overseas home.

Resources

Books

Many informative and helpful books designed to help spouses cope with the challenges of successful living abroad have been published since mine first appeared in 1992. There are far too many for me to give a comprehensive list, so I have listed some of my favourites. It is also worth taking the time to check out publishers who specialize in expatriate topics, such as Intercultural Press, Nicholas Brealey Publishing, and Explorer Publishing.

Ashman, Anastasia M., & Gökmen, Jennifer Eaton (Eds.). 2006. *Tales from the Expat Harem: Foreign Women in Modern Turkey.* Seal Press.

Barkhouse, Danielle. 2008. *The Expat Arc: An Expat's Journey Over Culture Shock.* Create Space.

Bryson, Debra, & Hoge, Charise M. 2005. *A Portable Identity: A Woman's Guide to Maintaining a Sense of Self while Moving Overseas.* Transition Press International.

Copeland, Anne. 2005. *Global Baby.* Interchange Institute.

Hess, Melissa Brayer, & Linderman, Patricia. 2007. *The Expert Expat: Your Guide to Successful Relocation Abroad* (Rev. ed.). Nicholas Brealey Publishing.

Keenan, Brigid. 2005. *Diplomatic Baggage: The Adventures of a Trailing Spouse.* John Murray.

Malewski, Margaret. 2005. *GenXpat: The Young Professional's Guide to Making a Successful Life Abroad.* Intercultural Press.

Parfitt, Jo. 2006. *Expat Entrepreneur: How to Create and Maintain Your Own Portable Career Anywhere in the World.* Lean Marketing Press.

———. 2007. *Expat Writer: Release the Book Within.* Lean Marketing Press.

———. 2008. *A Career in Your Suitcase* (3rd ed.). Lean Marketing Press.

Pascoe, Robin. 2000. *Homeward Bound: A Spouse's Guide to Repatriation.* Expatriate Press.

———. 2003. *A Moveable Marriage: Relocate Your Relationship without Breaking It.* Expatriate Press.

———. 2006. *Raising Global Nomads: Parenting Abroad in an On-Demand World.* Expatriate Press.

Pollock, David C., & Van Reken, Ruth E. 2001. *Third Culture Kids: The Experience of Growing Up Among Worlds.* Nicholas Brealey Publishing.

Roman, Beverly. 2006. *Home Away from Home: Turning Your International Relocation into a Lifetime Enhancement* (Rev. ed.). BR Anchor Books.

Tessen, Christina Henry De (Ed.). 2002. *Expat: Women's True Tales of Life Abroad.* Seal Press.

Van Reken, Ruth E. 1995. *Letters Never Sent: One Woman's Journey from Hurt to Wholeness.* Letters.

Weston, Marian. 2007. *Alone at Home: The Practical Guide for Coping Alone.* Swift Transitions.

Websites

Expat Women – www.expatwomen.com
An extremely comprehensive and informative site designed to help all expatriate women living outside of their home country. Whether you are a seasoned expat woman or one having your first experience living overseas, there is something for everyone on this site.

The Trailing Spouse – www.thetrailingspouse.com
The website of Yvonne McNulty, an academic in human resource management who has published extensively on spousal issues as they relate to mobility.

Trailing Spouse Network –
www.ausmerica.com/blog/trailing-spouse-network
This is an informal community of expat professionals whose purpose is to facilitate communication and collaboration on matters related to business and employment as part of the expat lifestyle.

Career in Your Suitcase – www.career-in-your-suitcase.com
One of several websites from expat author, publisher, and speaker Jo Parfitt. This site is for the book's third edition, to assist spouses searching for a career jump-start when they move abroad.

Career by Choice – www.careerbychoice.com
Website of career coach Megan Fitzgerald, to help expatriate professionals and entrepreneurs use their unique value or personal brand to build a career or business that fits who they are and their international lifestyle.

American Domestic Violence Crisis Line –
www.866uswomen.org
The mission of the American Domestic Violence Crisis Line is to serve Americans being abused in foreign countries. The crisis line number is toll free internationally by calling the local AT&T operator from the country you are living in and asking to be connected to 866-USWOMEN. The crisis line is toll free in the United States to serve families who have loved ones being abused overseas.

Federation of American Women's Clubs Overseas –
www.fawco.org
A complete listing of American women's clubs abroad to help women find an organization near them. Through FAWCO, you can find out about other local groups catering to your nationality.

Tales from a Small Planet – www.talesmag.com
This wonderful site, which began as a subversive e-zine for American foreign service spouses, offers, among other features, "real post reports" written by spouses in-country.

A Portable Identity – www.aportableidentity.com
The website of Debra Bryson and Charise Hoge, authors of *A Portable Identity: A Woman's Guide to Maintaining a Sense of Self While Moving Overseas* and expatriate coaches, who specialize in helping accompanying spouses take charge of change when life is turned upside down with a move.

School Choice International – www.schoolchoiceintl.com
School Choice International, owned by international school guru Elizabeth Perelstein, provides accurate, timely information and practical strategies to solve the educational needs of relocating families anywhere in the world.

About the Author

Robin Pascoe is well known to travelling spouses internationally for her humorous, compassionate, and encouraging presentations to expatriate communities, human resource groups, and corporate gatherings around the world. As well as writing countless articles and making many media appearances, Robin is the author of five books on the subject of global living and adjustment. Her personal experiences of packing and unpacking her life, marriage, and family throughout Asia were the inspiration for exploring the challenges and joys inherent to the expatriate lifestyle. Her popular website, ExpatExpert.com, is a treasure trove of information, opinion, and humour for expatriate families. Robin currently lives in North Vancouver, Canada.

Praise for Robin's Previous Work

"Just knowing that there was someone out there who empathized and would write loads of reassuring e-mails to me was a real lifeline for me. Your total honesty is such an icebreaker and really resounds with any expatriate who is struggling. Keep up the good work."
—*Marian Weston, author of* Alone at Home

"Robin Pascoe is exactly what her brand promises, that is, the 'expat expert.' She is always willing to share her knowledge, experience, and importantly her contacts, to help others in the relocation field. Robin is definitely a highly respected go-to person in the expat industry. She's a legend."
—*Andrea Martins, Director & Co-founder, ExpatWomen.com*

"Your approach to 'raising global nomads' was a tremendous source of help and relief to what we are doing with our three children and the challenges they are facing in Peru."
—*By e-mail via ExpatExpert.com*

"I really appreciate your being there. Your 'rescue mission' for any woman like me is very generous, human, and honourable."
—*By e-mail via ExpatExpert.com*

"I heard you speak yesterday about *A Moveable Marriage* and wanted to thank you for making me feel so 'normal'! If only I had known that everything I have been experiencing is so common and I am not losing my mind after all."
—*By e-mail via ExpatExpert.com*

"Thank God for your website. I am an American living in Africa for six and a half years now. Every time I come home (to the U.S. about twice a year) I am finding it harder and harder to readjust. I'm home for my daughter's wedding just now and just needed a little support. I ran across your website and I'm thrilled to find others to relate to my expat experiences. Thank you!"
—*By e-mail via ExpatExpert.com*

"I wish to thank you for your contributions to my ever increasing knowledge on becoming an expat. I have just completed your book *Raising Global Nomads* and found it very helpful as we prepare our family for our first international assignment. I know now that I will make mistakes, but it makes me feel better to realize even the 'expert' had low days too."
— *By e-mail via ExpatExpert.com*

"Robin Pascoe is definitely my hero! Have I told you how many times I have referred friends to her advice and book? I have reread several chapters . . . It is so comforting to know that others have felt the same as I do . . . transition is a very long process!"
— *By e-mail via ExpatExpert.com*

"I found your site and read *A Moveable Marriage* last spring. I love the sage and humorous advice you offer in it and found the book helpful in just looking at and dealing with life with a husband who travels frequently and the frustrations with communication and understanding that brings. I laughed out loud and even welled up a few times thinking about the future."
— *By e-mail via ExpatExpert.com*

"It is clear that Robin Pascoe's goal in *Homeward Bound* is not to discourage people from the enriching experience of being a globally nomadic family, but rather to be better prepared to do it well and gain the greatest benefits from the experience. This is a book written from both the head and the heart, and it speaks to the head and the heart of the reader."
—*David Pollock, co-author of* Third Culture Kids

Printed in the United States
152241LV00001B/9/P